SERMON AT THE COUNCIL OF BENEVENTO

Pope Victor III
Bishop of Rome

Translated by: D.P. Curtin

Copyright @ 2009 Dalcassian Press LLC

All rights reserved. No part of this publication may be reproduced, distributed, or transmitted in any form or by any means, including photocopying, recording, or other electronic or mechanical methods, without the prior written permission of the publisher, except in the case of brief quotations embodied in critical reviews and certain other non-commercial uses permitted by copyright law. For permission request, write to Dalcassian Press LLC at dalcassianpublishing at gmail.com

ISBN: 979-8-8693-3392-6 (Paperback)

Library of Congress Control Number:
Author: Curtin, D.P. (1985-)

Printed by Ingram Content Group, 1 Ingram Blvd, La Vergne, Tennessee

First printing edition 2009.

SERMON GIVEN IN THE SYNOD OF BENEVENTO

Your love, dear brothers of the co-bishops (and let not the whole world hide it), the holy Roman and apostolic see, which I serve under God's authority, knows how many adversities it has endured, how many in short the trapezium has been broken by hammers and hammers by the heresies of Simonia, so much so that the column of the living God seemed to be swaying almost shaken , and the boats of the great fisherman were broken up by the swelling waves, and perished by the fate of the shipwreck. For Guibert, the heresiarch, who, during the lifetime of my predecessor Pope Gregory of holy memory, invaded the Roman Church, the forerunner of the Antichrist and the standard-bearer of Satan, does not cease to scatter, slaughter, and fleece the sheep of Christ.

For having become an instigator and an instigator of evils, who can relate how many injuries Pope Gregory inflicted, what persecutions, how many defeats he inflicted? The author of the conspiracy himself stirred up the conspirators against him; he fled from the city; the priesthood, as far as it was in him,

SERMON AT THE COUNCIL OF BENEVENTO

Simoniacus prevailed and persevered, stirred up the Roman empire against him, stirred up nations and kingdoms; and (which is unheard of for ages) he himself, having been excommunicated and condemned, presumed to excommunicate the holy pontiff, until now he did not cease to desecrate the Roman city with sacrileges, murders, perjury, conspiracies, crimes, and all kinds of vices; evoking an abominable deed, forced by the emperor's army, the invader of the apostolic seat was effected against the precepts of the Gospel, against the decrees of the prophets and apostles, against the law of the canons and Roman pontiffs, without the prior judgment of the cardinal bishops, without the approving vote of the Roman clergy, without the required consent of the devout people in the holy Roman Church it is the chief effect of all wickedness and perdition. But by the power of Almighty God, when the aforesaid pontiff Gregory, after many labors and struggles, had called him to eternal rest, and by the unanimous agreement of the bishops and the provincial cardinals and the elders, together with the Roman clergy and people, had presided over our smallness in every way contradicting and resisting the apostolic see, not fearing the judgment of the eternal emperor. even now he does not cease to persecute Christ and his sheep, for whom he shed his blood. Therefore, by the authority of God and of the blessed apostles Peter and Paul, and of all the saints, we deprive him of all priestly office and honor, and, separating him from the thresholds of the Church, bind him with the bond of anathema.

Moreover, you know and well know what tricks they have devised, and how much pressure Hugh, the archbishop of Lyons, and Richard, the abbot of Massili, have brought to bear on me. And indeed, Richard of Rome had effected our election with the cardinals and bishops: but Hugh, coming to us a little after, with a heavy footstep, while he offered us the obedience due to the supreme pontiff unwilling and recanting, had demanded and received an embassy from us in the parts of Gaul. Therefore, until they saw that our littleness was contrary to the choice made and approved by them, they themselves insisted by all means that we should not throw off the burden imposed on us for the benefit of the Church. But when at last they saw us yielding, the furnace, exhausted by the flame which had been conceived for a long time, vomited out. Therefore, seeing that the unanimity of all the brothers was constantly struggling, they were separated from each other and ours by continuous communion. Whence it happened to you that the apostolic parties had either heard or seen me, I will endeavor to conclude with two other letters, dear life. And in order to remove from the readers every scruple of doubt, I have connected each and every person by whom these things have been related to me: considering it better to keep silent altogether, than to tell something false or untruthful.

Theophilus When the Scripture says: The mouth that lies kills the soul (Wis. 1:11), why did the blessed Paul, who was freed from the prison guard together with Silas, claim to be a Roman, when it is more clearly established that he was not a Roman, but a Jew?

You desire: Let this be far from the hearts of the faithful, that the preacher of truth, and the teacher of the nations, should be believed to have committed a lie in someone! For the most blessed Paul was both a Roman, and he was not a Roman; He was not a Roman, because he had not come from a Roman city. He was indeed a Roman, because all the Jewish people, like almost the whole world, lived under the dominion of the Roman Empire at that time. Or even for the reason that he is interpreted as a high Roman, he could very appropriately and justly call himself a Roman, because he in no way hesitated that he was high, as he says: "But our conversation is in the heavens" (Phil. 3).

Theophilus, I confess, I am very pleased with what you say, but please begin to tell me what you promised.

Desire It is a very new matter which I am relating, and confirmed by the assertion of our elders concerning the most reverend man: Appollinare, namely, the abbot of our monastery, to whom, God the supporter, I may serve unworthy; One day, when, compelled by necessity, he was looking for the lands of the monastery, he came to the river Lirim; and when there was a lack of a ship by which he could cross the river, full of faith, fortifying himself with the sign of the holy cross, he came to the bank of the river, and, clothed as he was, and with shoes on his feet, entered the river; and so the trail reached the other bank, so that not even his shoes were seen to be wet. Observe, I pray you, how much holiness, and how much religion and merit with Almighty God this man was, who, still weighed down by the weight of his body, was allowed to walk on a liquid element as if on a dry one; so that the prince of the apostles may be considered in this deed, when the waves from above, at the command of the Lord, were thus stepped on.

Theophilus I have certainly observed and greatly marvel when in our times, in which, according to the prediction of the Prophet: The saint has failed, truths have diminished from the sons of men; there is no one who does good, not even one (Ps. 13) Almighty God has deigned to do such things.

Desire If you pay attention, dearest brother, to what the Lord deigned to promise his disciples: Behold, I am with you always until the end of the age (Matt. 28), you will be able to rejoice rather than wonder.

Theophilus And indeed I rejoiced, and greatly rejoiced; but I beseech you to continue what you have begun.

Desire At the same time, when the nation of the Agarenes, led by a fleet, had largely ravaged Italy, how Almighty God had delivered this monastery from their hands, I did not think it worthy to pass by in silence. When, therefore, they had consumed everything around with fire and steel, they also plundered the churches of the most holy Peter and Paul. Then the Appians, setting out on their journey, attacked the city of Fundana, burned it with fire, and killed or captured all those who dwelt in it. And when they departed from thence, and applying to the neighborhood of our monastery across the river Lirim, for night was already threatening the land, they encamped, that in the morning they might utterly destroy every monastery, or carry away as booty whatever they could find there; and as they were exceedingly thirsty for blood, brothers, let them cut their throats with the sword. And when this so terrible, so great, and so fearful a danger was announced in the monastery, all the brethren were struck with exceeding terror, and were terrified, praying emphatically to the divine majesty, that he would deign to graciously receive their souls, whose bodies had died so suddenly and so fearfully, due to their demanding sins. for they believed that they would no longer live in this world, who saw the sword of death so near threatening them. Therefore, when their heads had been sprinkled with ashes throughout the night, and they were engaged in vigils and prayers, the most reverend man, the abbot of Apollinaris, whom I have mentioned above, spoke to the abbot of Bassatius, a religious man of course, by a vision, saying: Do not be afraid, lest you be saddened; for at this time you will not be captured by the Agarenes, nor will they be able to inflict any damage on you with the divine protecting right hand; but the more they return, the more they will attempt to go to the borders; but you will henceforth remain safe and unharmed, because the most holy Father Benedict has obtained your salvation from the Almighty Lord; for he himself comes to help you, and us all together with him. Therefore, the venerable man Bassatius, abbot, awoke from his sleep, called his brethren together, and reported what he had seen, and what had been revealed to him; and he exhorted them to implore the almighty Lord urgently. But they, certain of divine mercy, were excited, praising and blessing the Lord, and finished the rest of the night with prayers and prayers. But the air was so serene, that not even a thin cloud could be seen in it, when suddenly the sky thickened with clouds, the thunder crackled, flashes of lightning and lightning flashed frequently, and so much rain poured down on the earth that the river Liris, overflowing widely, seemed like a sea. Therefore, at daybreak, the barbarians, rising from their camp, approached the bank of the river, searching more diligently to see if by any chance they could find a boat and a ford, so that they might be able to cross the river. , had remained empty, burning the cells of our monastery across the Lyris, they turned to the army and began to leave as quickly as possible. And when they had arrived at that place, where the aforesaid river Lirus flows into the open mouth of the sea, they left all the horses they had, weakened by the blows, and having their nerves cut, because they could not carry them with them. They, however, having embarked in ships, and giving canvas to the winds, and plowing their aqueducts in a straight course, had arrived at Sicily, and hoped to find themselves speedily dry. And when they were anxiously questioned by them, where did they rush so joyfully, so cheerfully, or so burdened? They professed to come from Italy and boasted that they had delivered everything there to fire and steel: even the houses of Peter and Paul, and also of Benedict. And you, they say, who are you, who dare to question us so earnestly, so diligently, and so curiously? We, they say, are called one Peter, the other Benedict, whose houses you boasted of having invaded; but whose power and whose power we are, let us experience as soon as possible. And having said these things, they were taken away from their sight.

SERMON AT THE COUNCIL OF BENEVENTO

Soon, therefore, with furious winds on every side, and swelling waves, such a storm suddenly arose that all the ships either collided with each other or were driven to pieces by the rocks. So that out of all that multitude of heathens scarcely a few remained who could have told the citizens these things, by whom they had been sent. And it is true that Almighty God allowed his churches to be devastated by them for a time, but he did not suffer them to be congratulated any longer on such a deed. This fact seems to me to have been fulfilled, which blessed P. Benedict had once promised his disciples, saying: I am present to you, beloved children, laying aside the burden of the flesh, and being your constant co-operator through the grace of God. That also which the Lord brought to B. Peter, saying: You are Peter, and on this rock I will build my church, and the gates of hell will not prevail against it (Matt. 16). He does not say, they will not be strong; but they will not prevail: for the gates of hell are the pagans, the heretics and the Jews, who then seem to be strong against the Church of God, when the Lord allows his faithful to be scourged through them; but they will not prevail, because the almighty and merciful God does not allow them to have perpetual triumphs over his Church. Hence also the apostle exhorts, saying: We suffer tribulation, but we are not constrained; we are encouraged, but we are not discouraged; we suffer persecution, but we are not abandoned; we are humbled, but not confounded; we suffer, but we do not perish (2 Cor. 4).

Theophilus, I really like what you have to say.

Desire John, a priest of holy memory, who for some time held the office of dean in our monastery, was later in charge of your monastery which was built within the city of Lucense, and of how much obedience and humility he was, many monks who knew him and who are still alive are witnesses. Of the wonderful things which the divine majesty deigned to work through him, because many things have slipped from my memory, which I recall, I will relate a few. When the same man of God was devoted to fastings, vigils, prayers, and most of all to the generosity of alms, he earned so much grace by shedding tears to the Lord, that there was no doubt that those tears, which had been issued from such a simple and humble heart, would have been able to obtain much from God. And when the fame of his sanctity spread throughout the same city, a certain demoniac, who was severely tormented, was brought to the monastery over which he was in charge. And when she had been bound by great prayers by those who had taken her, that she might pray to the Lord for him, she entered the oratory with the brothers called together, and with many tears poured out prayers to the Lord for her, and immediately the demon fled from her.

But I will not cease this, which I have acknowledged to truthful men talking about the same venerable man, which is indeed so clear, that it is hidden or unknown to almost no one who dwells within the walls of the aforesaid city of Lucknow. For the wife of a certain illustrious man lay in bed, seized with infirmity, and she was brought to such extremes by growing weakness, that for three days she lay senseless and speechless, as though she were dead. And when all who were present utterly despaired of her life, it was sent to the man of God, that he might deign to offer sacrifices and prayers for her to the Almighty Lord. But he, as he was benevolent in heart, and ready to the prayers of the supplicants, soon dressed in priestly garments, came to the altar to offer sacrifice to Almighty God. Therefore, when his name was mentioned during the sacred solemnities of the masses, she answered in her own house, far from the monastery, from the bed in which she lay as if lifeless, as if she were called by someone. And when she was asked by those who were present what she had said, or to whom she had given the answer, she said: Is not Lord John in charge here? for he himself called me, and I answered him. But they were astounded by so unusual, so famous, and so astonishing a miracle, and also because they saw her, who had lain almost lifeless, almost healthy and unharmed; and because he reported having heard his voice when he was so far away, they immediately took care to send messages to the monastery, that they might recognize what the servant of God was doing, and tell them: believing without doubt that the woman had not risen from bed so quickly, and had given an answer. And when those who had been sent had entered the oratory of the monastery, they found the man of God standing near the altar, and offering a sacrifice to the Lord, the author of the distance. and noting the hour minutely, they found that at the same moment, when the solemnity of the mass had been recited, she had risen from bed, and had given her answer.

There was also a most eloquent and learned man of happy memory, St. Alexander the Pope: who first ruled Lucense, and afterwards the Roman Church, from whose mouth I happened to hear what I am now relating about the same venerable man. When at a certain time the same aforesaid pontiff was gravely ill, seized with a fever, and every day growing more violently tired, he suddenly remembered that he had often heard a popular report about the aforesaid servant of God: namely, that whoever was seized with a fever had drunk from the water that flowed from his hands, while after the hymns of the masses would be washed away, and he would soon be freed in good health. He therefore secretly sent those who should have brought him some of that water. And when those who had been sent had brought him the water he had asked for, he soon drank, and so suddenly was he restored to his former health, that no signs of that infirmity remained in him.

Another man also of venerable life, Guinizzo by name, was a monk in mind and habit, who, coming from our further Spain to the convent, led a solitary life for a considerable time in this neighboring forest, ending his life everywhere in the service of the almighty Lord Jesus Christ. About which venerable man John, abbot of the monastery of St. Vincent, situated near the source of the river Vulturni, who was very familiar to him, was wont to relate many things that surprised me, when he was still in charge of the prefect in our monastery. There was a disciple of whose name Januarius, a monk of great obedience and great abstinence. Aquinas, who had been sent by his master, the venerable Guinizzo, to repair the ironwork with which they were accustomed to work, went to the blacksmith's house, and demanded of him that the same ironwork be repaired for a fee. The blacksmith, however, began to mock him, saying: Is this solitary man so ruddy and fat from bread and water? This blush, as it seems to me, comes more from wine than from drawn milk. And he said: Today, he said, I will show you whether I am flushed with redness from nature or from constant drinking of wine. But when the iron which had been put into the fire was boiling fiercely, and the smith, taking it with tongs, had placed it on the anvil, and the sparks, flying hither and thither, had lit up almost the whole house, the iron fell by chance from the anvil to the ground. Then the venerable man Januarius, seeing that the iron had fallen from the anvil, stooping down, held the hot iron with his bare hand, and placing it on the anvil, urged the hammerer to strike it as quickly as possible. But those who were present, having seen so great a miracle, were greatly terrified, and, throwing themselves at his feet, humbly begged pardon for the mockery they had inflicted on him. And so it came to pass that all that derision was turned into veneration, which foolish men had presumptuously presumed to inflict upon the servant of God. And so when the venerable man had therefore returned to the master, and to the cell, he was vehemently rebuked by him, because, yielding to those who insulted him, he had presumed to do such things in the eyes of men. And when he was asked how he knew this, or who had told him: He, he said, who promised you that you might do it, also told me that I might know it.

Theophilus When the Lord says: Let your light shine before men, that they may see your good works and glorify your Father who is in heaven (Luke 12), what is it that holy men hide their good things, and so that they may not be seen by some, they work hard?

Desire Although holy men sometimes display their works in public, their intention remains in secret; for by what they do inwardly, they do not require praise outwardly, because they also desire to set an example of good work to their neighbors, and yet, through the intention with which they desire to please God alone, they always wish it to be secret. Then, I say, they desire to conceal their possessions, when they see that no profit of souls, no profit of fraternal salvation, will come from their disclosure. But when they see from this that they can gain something for the glory of Almighty God, then they allow their goods to be declared and publicized, because they do not require the praise of their own, but of their Creator.

Theophilus The reason is clear enough, and I do not think that anything more is required from it.

Desire also, what he is accustomed to relate about this excellent man, that is to say Guinizzo, John the religious monk, who resides in this neighboring forest under the discipline of an anchorite, I have thought worthy to associate with this little book of ours; for he said: Because when he was still living in his monastery in the city of Benevento, one day a certain servant of God brought it to him and to the other brothers who were there, saying: You must know for certain that today a great man from among the monks at Mount Casinus has passed from this world to the Lord. When they heard this, they were amazed that he could see his soul coming out of his body for nearly eighty miles, and not using faith, they endeavored to trace it with precision. And on that day, it was discovered that that venerable man had given up his soul, by which the aforesaid servant of God recognized that he had been placed in Benevento.

But I will not be silent about this, which I recognized in reference to the brothers of the monk Mancus, whom I myself saw placed in the monastery, and who has already died in our time. When he had come hither from the parts of Apulia by the grace of conversion, he was received by our predecessor, Richard, the abbot, and joined the congregation of the brethren. And so, in the monastery in body, dwelling in the world in mind, he always meditated on earthly things: all the mastery of regular training seemed to him burdensome and importunate. Then he began to ask permission from the abbot, and to find many opportunities by which he could visit his country and his parents. And when he had been repeatedly admonished by his abbot, that he should take the path of truth, which he had once taken, to lead it in a better way day by day to the end, laying aside all sluggishness and laziness, he should study the utmost, lest, according to the sentence of the Lord (Luke 9:62), he should plow holding and looking back, he could not be fit for the kingdom of heaven; and lest, imitating Lot's wife, turning to the statue of salt (Gen. 19:16), he should present a horrible spectacle to all: nevertheless he (whose mind had once been besieged by evil) did not rest in any way, but by tiring the abbot and his brothers with prayers every day, that they would allow him to return to his country. he demanded in every way. And when he saw that his hope of return was frustrated, he left the monastery secretly, and, after the manner of a fugitive slave, seizing the darkness of the night, like a dog to his vomit, he returned to his country, incited by the devil, and remaining in the house of his parents, he began to live there secularly, as he had long conceived in his mind. But when he had been repeatedly warned by his abbot by message to return to the walls of the monastery, and he, disregarding the salutary warnings, neglected to obey, he was deprived of communion by the same abbot. When, therefore, not many days later he was lying in bed, seized with a little sickness, he saw a huge lion entering the door and coming towards him with an open mouth. But he, terrified at the entrance of the wild beast, began to cry out with a loud voice, saying: Run, run, for this lion is about to devour me. But Leo, roaring, rushed upon him, and biting, seizing his hip, drew from it the largest piece of flesh, and thus disappeared, leaving him lying and seedless. And when many came together, astonished at the cry of that voice, they did not see a lion at all, but found the monk prostrated on the ground, lying and seedless. And so, when they raised him from the ground, with a little recovered spirit, he spread in order all that had happened to him, and he besought his relatives and neighbors that they might return to the monastery as soon as possible. His relatives, therefore, obeying his wish, carried him to the cell of this monastery of ours, which is situated opposite the town of Asculanus, and there after a little recovering his health, he returned to this monastery, and having accepted penance for the guilt he had committed, he lived for many years afterwards in the habit of holy conduct.

Theophilus This monk, as I see, was therefore handed over visibly for a time to the lion, that is, to the devil, so that afterwards he might deserve to be delivered invisibly from his power forever.

Desire Do you also want me to tell you how Almighty God always rescued this monastery from the hands of tyrants, and protected it from the invasion of enemies, by the merits of the blessed P. Benedict, with the right hand of his divinity?

Theophilus Tell me anything, for I promise to listen to all these things with an eager heart, a devout mind, and attentive ears.

Desire Pandulph Capuanus, the prince, was a most powerful and rich man, who, by robbing, shedding human blood, cruelly taking away cities, towns, and the estates of others, who remained around him, submitted to his dominion; practiced Therefore, when he had plundered most of the wealth of the churches of Christ, he took away all the camps, villages, and estates of this monastery led by the sacrilegious greed, so that not a single peasant who cultivated the fields, or the fields that were cultivated by the peasants, was left to the monks. Moreover, he carried away all the treasure of this monastery, and in a citadel, which he had built not far from the city of Capua, on the mountain

SERMON AT THE COUNCIL OF BENEVENTO

called St. Agatha the Martyr, in which he had brought many spoils of orphans, widows, churches, and the poor, and deposited them. But since the Almighty God would have put an end to so many crimes, and the tears and voices of orphans, widows, and the poor, as well as the prayers and supplications of God's servants, would have been accepted in the sight of his Divinity, as it is written: The king's heart is in the hand of God (Prov. 21:1); He inspired the mind of the emperor Conradi, to return to Italy and come to Rome (in 1038) to vindicate his churches and rescue Italy from the hands of tyrants. When, therefore, he had assembled a great army and entered Rome, entering Italy, he decided to send the best men of his side to Capua, to Prince Pandulph, to whom, in order that the goods of St. Benedict had been unjustly taken from him, he would, after any delay, restore them, and the nobles or men of any kind, whom they had captured and greatly He would detain many in prison, bound with the weight of iron, release them, and return all their property to them speedily; he wished to rule by the same men; for the desire to come to these parts was not in the least in his mind, if he could accomplish those things which he had ordered to Pandulph through the aforesaid men. But the Almighty God, who hardened Pharaoh's heart because of the many evils he had inflicted on God's people without cause, so that he would not believe his servant Moses who was showing miraculous signs and wonders (Ex. 10:1), also hardened his heart so that he would not obey the command of the emperor. And when those who had been sent by the emperor had come to Capua, having had many words with the same Pandulph in vain, they returned to the emperor without effect. But when the emperor saw that he was despised by the prince, moved with anger, he marched out of Rome with his army, came to Casinum, and went up to the threshold of BP Benedict. When the hour had come, he entered the chapter of the brothers, and, gathering together, he asked the brothers to pray to the Lord for him; and there before them the blessed and blessed God testified that he had come to these parts for no other reason than to rescue his monastery from the hand of a most cruel tyrant. Then, with the benediction, he entered Capua from there; but the companions of the aforesaid prince, who were detaining the goods of the monastery for their own use, when they had learned of the arrival of Augustus, they were all scattered, fleeing hither and thither. And so it happened that the monastery received back all the camps, villages, and estates that had been taken from it in one day, and those which had been gathered there for the other use of the ministers of crimes came into the power of the monks. It seems to me that that which Benedict had once predicted to his disciples who were saddened by the want of bread: That today they may have less, but tomorrow they may have abundance. Therefore, the aforesaid Augustus entered Capua, taking away the honor of the leadership of Pandulph, and appointed another in his place. But he himself, fleeing from the same city, betook himself to the citadel which he had fortified on the mountain of St. Agatha the Martyr with great diligence. Wherefore by the divine arrangement it happened that all that he had acquired during the course of time by robbing, perjuring, and shedding the innocent blood of many, he lost in the space of one week: and nothing remained to him of the many and many municipalities he had acquired, except the citadel which we have foretold, and who had many children born to his own having taken things away, he forced them to beg, and those who have sprung from him continue to beg here and there to this day. Who doubts that all these things happened to him through the merits of B. Benedict, whose goods he himself, led by the lust of an unjust leader, destroyed.

Theophilus, there is no doubt about this matter, when the aforesaid emperor testified before his brothers that he crossed Rome for no other reason than the defense of the monastery of Saint Benedict.

Desire At another time (in the year 1049) a certain Capuan, Pandulph by name, having collected from his friends and neighbors horsemen from all quarters, and with a not small number of soldiers, attempted to attack and capture the fortress of this monastery called Concha, inciting the devil. He set out from the city of Capua with his followers, when the day was already approaching evening, so that, walking through the whole night, before daybreak, while all were still safely asleep there, he might be able to attack and take the aforesaid fortress. But when they had left the city, they had proceeded a little, and had come to that place, from which they had decided to walk no longer in the day, but in the night, so as not to be seen by any, when they had lingered there a little, the desired night came on. Who, like children of darkness, caring more for darkness than for light, and what the Lord says in the Gospel: He who walks in the night stumbles (John 11), paying no attention at all, began to walk through the field of one farm and hasten as fast as possible to the invasion of the aforesaid camp. So, the horses, with their bloody shoes, thinking that they were going on a straight course, ran all night round the aforesaid field. But in the morning, by the wonderful disposition of God's work, they found themselves there where the night had taken them; and thus, frustrated, confused, and wonderfully tired of what they desired, they returned to their home empty.

At another time also, while the fishermen of this monastery had cast their nets into the sea to catch fish for the refreshment of the brethren, a certain Northman, swollen in mind and puffed up with pride, furious in spirit, came up, and, as they are eager for robbery, insatiably anxious to invade other people's goods, was arrested one of the fishermen took off the garment in which he was clothed, and immediately put it on himself; then entering the boat, he began to compel the fisherman to bring out the nets from the deep, so far as to carry away the fish that were found in them, taking away with him. And when the fisherman refused and said that he wished to take the fish for the monks, and not for the Normans' refreshment, he was severely beaten by the same Norman and thrown into the sea. But when the same Norman, eager for the prey of fish, had begun to draw the nets from the deep by himself, and to gather the fish, he suddenly fell from the boat, and being stopped by the sea, breathed his last. But, what a wonderful saying! before him the wave threw him dead on the shore, which the fisherman, who had been thrown into the waters by it, could have reached by swimming alive.

At another time also, robbers having entered the cellar of this monastery of ours in the night, had stolen meat, cheese, and lard, and filled their sacks with it; but when they went outside, they tried to lift the bags which they had filled, but they could not at all; then, leaving behind their baggage, they tried to escape, and during the whole night they walked this way and that through the walls of the monastery, but were never able to get out. Therefore, in the morning, when they saw themselves within the walls of the monastery, terrified by fear and conscious of their guilt, they did not know what to do. At last, finding a plan among themselves, they went out by the gate of the monastery, if by any means they could escape, as if they were seen to have done no harm, the rest, who were going out of the monastery to do any work, mingled with each other, and with a slow foot, lest any suspicion should arise among them, took their way. They had stopped not far from the monastery. Meanwhile, when the storekeeper was about to provide the brothers with their usual wages, he entered the storeroom, found the sacks filled before the entrance, and being surprised, and not knowing what they were, demanded what was stored. But when he saw that the stores had been taken away, he was troubled by the loss, and went out, and found whatever he had lost in the very bags. He, greatly astonished, and already understanding what was happening, immediately summoned two or three boys to him, and took care to send them along the path leading down the mountain, if by chance they could find the chessmen who had admitted it. And when they had completed their orders, when they had left the monastery and had proceeded a little, they found them standing close by on the very path of the mountain. And when they had almost passed them, and had no suspicion of them, because they were known, they quickly completed the journey they had taken. But they, divinely terrified and driven as if mad, began to cry out after them and say: We know, lords, that you have come to arrest us; but have mercy on us; for we took nothing from thence, but having taken everything, we left it at the very entrance of the cellar. But when they heard these things, they seized them, tied them behind their backs by the hands, led them to the monastery, and presented them to the brethren, as they were bound with chains. Moreover, there were some who were less cautious about the commandment of the Lord, they were killed and judged to be dismissed in this way; but the rest, whose mind was pious in the Lord, and more diligently studying the commandments of God to fulfill the commandments of the Lord, having their bonds loosed, and being refreshed with food and drink, allow their children to depart. Oh, the wonderful kindness of the Lord Jesus Christ, the wonderful piety, the wonderful patience that he taught; since it is written in the Law (Lev. 19; Matt. 5): You shall love your friend and hate your enemy; nor is it commanded to render hand for hand, tooth for tooth, eye for eye, retribution for retribution; He wanted to command those who followed him to love his enemies, to do good to those who hated him, to greet those who did not greet him, to take off his coat, to let go of his cloak, and to return good things for bad things!

Theophilus, I am glad to admit that what you tell me is too much.

Desire It is a wonderful and exceedingly surprising thing, which I am about to tell, but it is so well known to so many people that no one should doubt it. At a certain time, therefore, Sergius, the master of the soldiers, who was in charge of the city of Neapolitan, was hunting on the very Sabbath of St. Paschal, going through the forest with his boys to catch a wild boar. but before the boar, fleeing from the net, was entangled in the snare, he was seized by the hunters, stabbed, and captured. But when the hour was already late, and the sun, going down to the west, had already almost cast a dark shadow over the land, the aforesaid commander of the soldiers, lest he should be occupied by the darkness of the night, taking what he had taken of the hunt, began to raid the house as fast as possible to everyone with his clients; He ordered only one boy, Pythagoras by name, to gather up his nets and follow him destructively. So, when the boy, who had been left behind, gathered his nets and followed his master along the straight path, suddenly two monks of a very reverent appearance presented themselves to him on the way. And when he was terrified with fear, he inquired who they were; they said: Fear not; just follow us. When, therefore, they were walking together for a little while through the same forest, they came to a certain swampy place of a very and terrible appearance; everywhere Pandulph the Capuan prince, of whom I have mentioned above, who had died not long before, is shown to him pitifully, bound with iron chains, and sunk up to his throat in the cesspool of that lake. Meanwhile, two black spirits, making twists from wild vines, bound him by the throat, and plunged him into the very depth of the lake, and drew him up again. And when they had done these things several times, the aforesaid boy Pythagoras, though his voice was trembling, addressed him, to tell him why he was allowing such things. He, however, weeping and wailing, immediately made such an answer to the words of the questioning boy, saying: Although, O boy, of my innumerable crimes, the most numerous and infinite punishment has been prepared for me, yet for no reason do I suffer this punishment which you see, except for the sake of the golden cup. whom I took away from the monastery of St. Benedict, led by sacrilegious greed, and even when I was dying, I neglected to return it to him. But I implore you, and through Jesus Christ, the Lord Savior of all, whose precepts I wretchedly despised, I have sunk into this abyss of death, I charge you to either go to Capua yourself to my wife, or send a message to her, and the tortures that I suffer, and to return the cup to the monastery of St. Benedict, he insinuates. But he said: What will it benefit, if I tell him? for not that I have seen you, or that you suffer such things, is to be believed by me. To whom he answered: This is a sign from my side, that Pandulph, son of Guala, has the cup itself as a pledge, and that, given the solids which we owed him, he should receive it, and restore to the monastery of St.

Benedict every delay which had been postponed; I beg you to insinuate to him quickly that you do not delay. After these words the vision was removed from his eyes. But as soon as the boy returned home, he was seized with an illness and died within a few days. But what he had seen, and what had been said to him, he revealed to all who came to him. Even Pandulph himself, who had the cup with him on account of the pledge, at this very time, for some reason I do not know, going to Naples, reported that he had heard all these things from the mouth of Pythagoras himself; through whom also the same Pythagoras told his wife at Capua all that he had seen of her husband, or that he himself had sent her. But she, consulting herself rather than her husband, paid back the price which her husband had arranged, and took care neither to receive the cup nor to return it to the monastery.

Theophilus It is very surprising and must be considered with great caution why Almighty God wanted to show such things to this boy, when he who was shown to him was not freed from punishment, or, with so many and so many crimes hidden, appeared to be tortured for only a golden cup.

Desire That this man was seen in punishments, and yet disdaining to return the cup to his wife, was not freed from punishments, but it was done by the just, though secret, judgment of Almighty God, and his pious and kind providence was brought to the notice of men, so that whoever heard these things should fear , and check the mind and hands from the robbers of the churches; that even before death he should not be allowed to repent, and after death he should not be willing to work for his parents and relatives for whom he is freed from punishment; and so let it be done that those who put aside the fear of God in their life and fear to commit it in no way deserve forgiveness in that life, who neglected to earn it in that life by good and holy works. But the fact that he appeared to be judged by the golden cup alone, without speaking to the rest of the criminals, is clearly given to understand how strongly, how terribly, and how miserably he was tormented for many others, and with immense crimes, when he was tortured so fiercely and cruelly by the robbery of the little cup. For we have reported above that Pythagoras said the same thing to the boy, that many and immense offenses had been prepared for him for others. But we are not much surprised that he who, when he saw him in executions, was immediately seized with sickness, and died not after much time, if we attend to what happened to Daniel, a man who was a truthful interpreter of dreams and dreams. for after the vision of the spiritual mysteries, he immediately fell ill, and for many days, as he himself testifies, fainted (Dan. 8). But if such and such a great man did not receive spiritual visions, but was immediately seized with sickness and was infirm for many days, what wonder if this boy, given over to worldly cares, pressed by carnal desires, could not bear the vision of spiritual things, but was detained by infirmity and came to the extremes? But in all these the divine judgments are more to be feared than sought. These things are great and unfathomable, as the Psalmist testifies, who says: Your judgments are many in the abyss (Ps. 35): as Paul also testifies, who says: O the height of the riches of the wisdom and knowledge of God! How incomprehensible are his judgments, and how traceable are his ways? For who knew the meaning of the Lord, or who was his counsellor? or who gave it to him first, and it will be repaid to him? For from him, and through him, and in him are all things: glory and dominion forever and ever. Amen (Rom. 11).

THE SECOND BOOK, in which the miracles performed by St. Benedict and other monks in the monastery of Casin with divine help are dealt with. However, as we had promised, I will begin to write a book, now a second, with the help of God: in which I will take care to conclude the rest that remain in this monastery, or by the monks of this holy convent wherever the miracles performed by divine mercy in these times, which meet our memory.

As I was still a layman, and within the years of my youth, I heard from many, while living in the city of Benevento, about John, then archdeacon of the same church of Benevento, and afterwards abbot of this St. Coenobius, I will not pass over in silence. Since the same John was descended from an illustrious lineage, and what is more important, living religiously and studying to please the Almighty Lord in every way, he was so loved by the clergy and people that after the death of the archbishop they all asked for him the high priesthood of the same city. There was another deacon in the same church, Alix by name, who aspired by all means to obtain the pontiff, and had no idea in what order he might attain it. But as long as the same John the archdeacon survived, he despaired of being able to reach the summit of such honor. And when these things were rolling in his mind every day, the vain thought did not allow him to rest. When, on a certain day, both of them had sat down in secret in a place, and no one else was with them, a conversation arose between them about the fragility of such a miserable life, about the delight of heavenly and eternal life, about the punishment of sinners, and about the eternal glory of the righteous. And so, they determined among themselves to leave the glory of this world, and to adopt the habit of holy conversation; and that they might be more faithful, they confirmed by an oath what they had determined. Then they decided the day on which they would go to the gates of B. Benedict at the castle Casinum, and under the rule of his mastership they would serve the Lord Jesus Christ. Therefore, when the appointed day had arrived, on which they were to set out on their journey, Alix, who had one thing in his mind and another in his mouth, said to John the archdeacon: Dearest brother, since there is still something left of my affairs, which I desire to order according to God, you, I beseech you , go ahead, and as soon as you have assumed the habit of holy conversation, send me a message; But the archdeacon, coming to the monastery of Blessed Father Benedict, as soon as he had assumed the sacred habit, sent word to his associate that they had decided that he had already submitted his neck under the rule of the holy institution, and that he himself should come speedily, as he had promised, to tell him. But as soon as he had heard these things, the effect of his eagerness, because he saw that he who was foremost in the church had withdrawn, he refused to approach him at all, and denied that he could enter so narrow a way. Then he strove with all his might to obtain the highest honor of the pontificate. But the Almighty and just God arranged otherwise than he had hoped. For when the emperor Otho had left Germany and entered Italy, after he had disposed of the Roman affairs, as he thought, he went to Benevento, to which Alix was so familiar, that the same Augustus ordered him to be elected pontiff, the Church refusing. Afterwards, however, the emperor, returning to Rome, asked the Roman Pontiff to consecrate him, and he sent the consecrated Benevento back; The emperor then, seized with a fever, died after some days by divine provision. He, however, returning to Benevento, did not even dare to approach the walls of the city, but when he was repulsed with that dishonor, the citizens elected another pontiff. Indeed, Almighty God did these things for the revenge of the evildoers, but the praise of the good, so that he who, led by the desire of honor, fraudulently endeavored to drive his brother from the Church, should himself be banished from his country, and end his life as an exile in foreign soil.

In addition to this, I heard the following from the venerable Leo, who died a few years ago, and from other veteran monks. When, therefore, the same John had completed some years in the monastery of the rule of the holy institution, he requested permission from his abbot. He went to Jerusalem and spent six consecutive years in the service of God on Mount Sinai. Afterwards, however, he remained for some time in Greece on the mountain called Hagionoros. But those things which happened to have seen him in that place, seem to me by no means to be withheld.

For a certain hermit, remaining on the same mountain, was either frequented by, or known to, a few. While one day the brother who ministered to him, and brought him food on certain days, had led the aforesaid venerable John to the same servant of God, as he was afterwards wont to report to his disciples with tears, he was kindly received by him, as was fitting, and with a speech between they were being talked about the joys of heavenly life longer, the servant of God said to those who had come: Come, brothers, for the hour is already here, let us take food for the body, so that when you return you will not fail on the way. And having said these things, he prepares the table, and sets out the meal. When, at last, the prayer had been made, and they had sat down to the table, a wonderful speech! A huge bear, coming from the neighboring forest, presented himself before the mouths of the boasters, carrying a honeycomb of sweet-flowing honey. And when they, greatly frightened, tried to take flight, that venerable hermit checked them and warned them not to be frightened, saying that it had been many years since the Almighty God had most often transmitted to him through that animal this gift of sweet nectar in his piety. So, when the meal was finished, they rose from the table, more satisfied in mind than in body, and with a perceived blessing, they returned to the monastery. Not many days later, however, the most blessed Father Benedict appeared to the same John in a vision and giving him the pastoral staff which he carried in his hand, warned Casinus to return as soon as possible to his monastery.

In the morning, therefore, to the abbot of the monastery, that is to say, to a religious man, he spread the vision which he had seen through the order. But he, as he was a prudent and discreet man, knowing the will of God in this vision, brought it in, saying: Brother John, make haste to return quickly to your monastery, lest you be seen to be so disobedient to the Father who appeared to you in a vision: for he has decreed that I it seems that Almighty God has placed you before his flock, and in his mercy has chosen you to feed his sheep faithfully. He, therefore, obeying the vision and admonition, and leaving the overseas field, with Christ as his guide, returned, and was placed in charge by the most pious man John, who was then in charge of the brethren, not long after (for the same abbot was already weak in body, and was unable to bear the weight of such a burden) was ordained abbot by the same venerable Father, by the counsel and election of the congregants of the brethren. But he, leaving the abbey, retired to a neighboring forest, and there, until the end of his life, he ended his life, dwelling in solitude in the care of the Almighty God.

Even what I heard about Felix, a monk of this monastery, must be passed over in silence. At a certain time, I do not know for what reason, it happened that I was in the city of Theatine, and when I was kindly and friendly received by the bishop and the clergy of that church, and by the grace of prayer they had led me to prayer, having done the prayer, I moved to the right of the church, and there the aedicula and the altar I looked And when I had asked the bishop and the clerics in whose honor that altar had been erected, the answer was that it was dedicated in honor of Blessed Felicity, the confessor of Christ. But when I inquired who that Felix was, they told me that he was a monk of the Cassinian congregation; and being sent by his abbot into those parts, that he might excel the shepherds, he ended his life there; and when the almighty God worked many wonderful things for his body, he was raised by his elders from the place in which he had previously lain, and was buried in this church, under this altar, as you see. Therefore, something memorable was told in that place that he had recently achieved, giving to the Almighty Lord.

When a certain blind man, stumbling his feet over all the obstacles, and was about to implore the merciful Lord, came before his altar, and prostrated with his whole body on the ground, with groans and sighs, prayed that he might have mercy on his merits, to the astonishment of all, he himself began to see with his own eyes the light which he had always longed to hear from others.

Theophilus, I would like to know if this venerable man, who was so famous, after his death in this life gave any sign of the merit of his life?

SERMON AT THE COUNCIL OF BENEVENTO

Desire Indeed, I did not find that this venerable man, while he lived in this world, gave any indication of his virtues; nevertheless, Almighty God is generally accustomed to act, so that those who seek to serve him with a devout mind, although in the flesh they show no sign of his holiness, yet after death whose merit have been, let it not be suffered to be concealed at all, so that while their extinct bodies are seen to glow with such miracles, human minds may be more keenly enkindled in his service.

Theophilus, I confess that I like what you say; but I beseech you, continue what you have begun; so that while I listen to what I greatly desire, my weary soul may be relieved for the love of the heavenly country.

Desire A certain Gregory, a monk of the highest religion, was said to be in this convent, who, as I remember hearing from most of the brethren of this place, while he remained in the present life, under the rule of monastic discipline, endeavored most vigorously to serve the Almighty Lord. And when he had passed from this world at the end of his life, such a fragrance of fragrance emanated from the place where he lay dead, that all the monastery suddenly the sweetness of that fragrance spread, as if in a corner of a house, miraculously. And while they were all surprised by the indescribable sweetness of that smell, and did not at all know what it was, a messenger suddenly came hurrying from the house of the sick, who reported that Gregory the monk had died. Almighty God therefore wished to show how great a man this man was, whose soul, when he went forth, filled the whole convent with such a wonderful fragrance.

Another one, as the brothers who still survive relate, was called Angelus, a monk in this monastery, whose life was certainly not unlike his name. While he had closed the last day of his bodily illness, the demoniac had indeed entered the kitchen. Benedict just did it for me; the soul of the angelic monk, because of the small hood which he wore on his head, he took away from me and brought it with him. And when all those who were present were astonished at his words and did not know what he was saying, suddenly the signal by which the death of the brothers is usually signaled sounded: and immediately all the brothers went hastily to the house of the sick, and found Angelus the monk already dead. In this matter it was clearly shown that he could not in any way harm the soul of that person, about whose death in the presence of his brothers the ancient enemy showed himself to be so sad and so mournful.

Theophilus Please tell me why the devil is so hostile to the human race, that from the beginning of his birth until the end of his life he works out in every way to turn man away from the commands of his Creator, and to lay all the traps he can for those who are heading for the eternal country.

Desire It is clear that the ancient enemy, who strives to equalize himself with his Creator, having suffered a great fall, has sunk into the abyss of a deep abyss; and that is why he exists contrary to the human race in every way, because he sees him ascending to that place, whence he himself, cast down by pride, has irretrievably fallen: it is from this that the noise, the maddening, the breaking in the passage of God's elect seem to be terrible.

Azzo was also a certain monk of a sufficiently religious life, who restored with all diligence the church of B. Michael the Archangel in the valley called Regis, built by Louis the Christian emperor with a wonderful work, but afterwards destroyed by the Saracens, and there he gathered the brethren to the service of Almighty God as he could. And when he had completed his years in the service of God there, and was almost at the end of his age, he returned to our monastery, whence he had been sent by his abbot. He who, being worn out by old age and disease, was lying in bed in the house of the infirm, drawing the last breath of his life, about to die, and many of his brethren, watching around his bed, chanting hymns and psalms, awaited his departure. But a certain brother, who still survives, and converses with us in the monastery, then a youth, but now a grand old man in age and manners, was resting in the dormitory with the rest of the brothers: when suddenly, looking up in the stormy night, he saw in a vision B. Michael the archangel, whose face the picture was teaching him he had recognized him coming through the dormitory: the other angel, following in his footsteps, was walking a little farther; looking at him, he said: Lord, are you not the archangel B. Michael? And he: Of course, I am. And he said: Sir, where are you going? To the house of the sick, said he, that I may take Brother Azzon with me, because it is now time, I am going on. And when he had said these things, the vision which he saw disappeared. He immediately awoke and went with haste to the house of the sick, and found his brother Azzon, who had already breathed his last from his body. In this matter it is clearly understood that the same Blessed Michael brought him with him, who testified that he had come to receive him.

A certain brother in our monastery was called Stephen the Venetian, who, coming from the parts of Venice, lived most earnestly in the habit of holy conduct, and the good of his humility, patience, and obedience was most clearly evident to all who were then gathered there in the service of Almighty God. And when it was already time for his worthy conversation to be rewarded by the most just Lord, he was burdened with bodily pain, placed before his brothers, and closed the last day. Then a certain very pious old woman, Agundia by name, a virgin in mind and body, who was in a saintly habit near the church of the Blessed Mary ever-virgin in the city founded around the foot of Mount Cassini, remained as usual before the clergy of the same city had risen to render nocturnal praises to God, before standing in the aforesaid church of the mother of God, he was praying to the Almighty Lord with groans, tears and sighs, when suddenly, looking back at the unseasonable hour of the night, he saw a pillar of fire from the cell, in which the sick brothers were accustomed to rest, coming out and reaching towards the sky. She immediately ordered the news to be sent to the monastery, who would diligently inquire if any of the sick brothers living in that cell had passed away from this world. Then he, who had been sent the messenger, perniciously ascended the mountain, entered the monastery, went to the house of the sick, and found Stephanus the religious monk dead: and on diligently inquiring, he found that he had given up his soul at that hour, by which a pillar of fire was seen by the maidservant of God to penetrate the poles.

Another certain one in our already mentioned monastery was called John of Venice, a monk of wonderful patience, obedience, and humility, who, after his death, made very clear his merits with the Lord Jesus Christ. When a certain brother, whose name is lost from memory, had by accident cracked his groin, so that his entrails, through a ruptured membrane, were falling between the flesh and the skin, he went to his tomb, and prostrated himself over it, with tears and groans, to pray to the Lord for him, from his inmost heart he demanded from his heart with emotion: believing without a doubt that he could receive health by his merits, who, placed in this life, strove to serve the Almighty Lord with all his strength. When, therefore, he had reclined for a little while in prayer over his tomb, he was so restored to health that it seemed that not even a trace of his former weakness remained in him.

The emerald monk, who still survives and resides in our monastery, reported to me what I am telling. He related that he had heard from the venerable priest Leo, his uncle of course, about Anthony the monk and priest. He who was not moderately educated in secular and divine literature, and who lived from his youth until the end of his life in a monastery of the same name, was known to almost everyone in this province. When, at a certain time, by an accident, as the aforesaid priest received from his mouth, he had broken down in a more secret place, and was greatly fatigued every day with increasing sickness, he was thinking to hire a physician, by whom he should be cut or burned, if he could by any means recover his health. He feared, however, that if he were to be cut by the doctor, as often happens, he might die, and again, if he were not cut, he would endure the pain, which is worse than death itself, and seemed to him more dangerous. Therefore, when he had been stirring these things within himself for some time, he believed that the only remedy for him was to go to the tomb of blessed Benedict and implore his mercy, hoping that he could be saved by his patronage, under whose teaching he had devoted himself most devoutly in his retirement. Immediately therefore he entered the church, and prostrating himself humbly before the altar, he prayed for a long time that Almighty God would deign to confer upon him the salvation of such a great Father. When he had finished his prayer, he rose from the floor on which he had been lying prostrate, and gathered some dust from the edge of the altar, and, binding it in a cloth, laid it over the place where he had suffered; .

I will take care to relate what I remember hearing from the brethren who still live in this present life, and who know him very well, concerning the holy conversation of Paul the monk. When the same Paul came to our convent for the sake of his salvation (in the year 1022), he was devoutly received by the abbot Theobald, a religious man, who was then most honorably in charge of the brethren. Whom the venerable Father commanded to dwell in the monastery of the blessed Father Benedict, which was built within the city of Capua: who, after he had arrived at the same place, so constrained himself under the rule of the holy institution, that for this reason he was considered wonderful by all. But the omnipotent, merciful and pious God, as much as his worthy conversation in this life pleased him, was pleased to show him after his death. For when he had spent some years in the same monastery practicing a religious life, honorable and worthy of God, he escaped from the prison of body and flesh at the command of the Lord, struck down by infirmity. Therefore, a certain venerable bishop, coming from the parts of Gaul, hastened for the grace of prayer to the church of Blessed Michael the Archangel, founded on Mount Cargano. And when he had come to the city of Capua, he was entertained near the church of the protomartyr Stephen. Finally, when he had risen from his bed in an untimely night, standing before the church of the aforesaid martyr, he was close to the ears of Almighty God with prayers and tears. And when for a long time he was amazed at the light which he saw, a signal sounded in the monastery, by which the exit of the brother was signified. He understood at once that among the number of his brothers some one of great merit had passed from this world, and at the same time had entered the sublime heights of heaven. So he immediately summoned the clergy and told what he had seen, and immediately sent a message to the monastery to identify who had died there. And when he who had been sent had entered the monastery, he found that the venerable monk Paulus had given up his soul from his body.

John, a very religious monk and priest, of whom I mentioned above, who, leaving the rule of the monastery, removed to the secret hermitage, remained in this neighboring forest in solitude until the end of his life; anxious to serve But here, in the time of Abbot Theobald, there had passed away from this light (in the year 1022), a certain monk named John, in the monastery of the Blessed Lawrence the Martyr, which is at Capua, was devoted most earnestly to the service of God: as usual, he had risen to pray to the almighty Lord, while standing with attentive mind praying to the merciful Lord, he suddenly looked up and saw a very bright light in the air and within the very soul of the venerable man John, penetrating heaven. Therefore, in the morning, desiring to know more certainly what he had seen, he came to Andrew, who was then in charge of the cells of this monastery, which is situated within the same city as Capua, and he reported what he had seen by order. He insisted on investigating the thing he had seen. He, endeavoring to comply with his wish, immediately sent word that he should carefully learn what had been said, and take care to return soon and tell it. Then the one who had been sent the messenger, while he was hastening on, and on the very journey, he met another coming from the monastery, who told the brothers who were staying in the aforesaid cell of Capua of the death of the aforesaid servant of God; from whom, inquiring minutely, he found that the aforesaid servant of God had been withdrawn from this light at that hour, by which John the religious monk, stationed at Capua, knew him to have miraculously entered heaven. Then both of them returned to those by whom they had been sent, the one reporting the death of the servant of God, and the other the vision which had been seen of him.

I learned these things from the testimony of many brothers, which I took care to record in our book. And although Peter, the venerable bishop of Ostiense, in his sermon, which he composed most lucidly to be read at the vigils of Blessed Father Benedict, inserted it elegantly and decently, yet among the other miracles which Almighty God to the praise of his name, even our memory, or of our elders, whom we ourselves saw, and to whom We acknowledged that he was deigned to show this in our monastery. Therefore, at a certain time from the beginning of the month of May until the end of the month of July, there was such a dryness of the air, that not even with the fewest drops the parched earth, and the frequent split cracks, seemed to be moistened in any way. Then one day a certain peasant, in order to set fire to the stubble of his wheat harvest in the field, so that he could cultivate the land more freely, carelessly set fire to it; and as soon as the fire, licking up the stubble, spread the flame on high, the breeze blew into the nearby forest, which lies beneath the monastery, and the peasant resisted it. Therefore, with the forest supplying him with infinite material, the fire running hither and thither along the sides of the mountain, every monastery was threatened with burning itself to ashes, while the people were watching on every side. When, therefore, the brothers, terrified and troubled with fear at the crackling of the flames, and roused in spirit, had risen from their beds (for this thing had happened to them while they were resting at noon), seeing so great and so sudden a danger, and not being able to think of how they could resist it, they at once went to the divine to contribute protections Therefore, with all their strength and from the innermost emotion of their hearts, they began to beseech the Almighty Lord, that by the merits of B. Father Benedict, in whatever order he wished, by his power he would rescue the monastery from the fire, which they completely despaired of being able to defend by human hands. And when some with their hands raised to heaven, and some with their bodies prostrate on the ground, some with their knees bowed, and others with their heads lowered to the ground, prayed to the Almighty Lord, suddenly a small cloud gathered itself on the side of this mountain, and spread over its summit, by divine commanding power; which soon produced such a shower of rain as to extinguish all the conflagration, and to save the monastery altogether. Let us endeavor, therefore, brethren, to live religiously and devoutly, and only to obtain the propitiation of our patrons, by serving God; by a good work, we have asked, we shall be delivered from the burning flame of vices, by the divine mercy granted.

At a certain time, as I have learned from those who knew him best, while the brothers of this monastery were building the church of the virgin B. Scholasticus within the city of Cajetan, in so far as they could have a shelter while they continued to buy some things there; some of the workmen on the top of the rock, which overlooks the sea at the head of the city, were breaking rocks with which the walls of the church were to be built. When he was more attentively pounding the same rocks with a hammer, the same hammer fell from the handle, and he fell over a huge precipice, which was open there, and fell into the sea. who, greatly saddened by the loss that had happened, came directly to the brothers where they were building the walls of the church, and mournfully reported what had happened to him. And when the hope of recovery had been taken away, and they had decided to make for themselves another hammer, with which to break the rocks for the building of the church, one of the brothers said: Let us go down there, brothers, perhaps B. Benedict will restore us the hammer by his merits, who once miraculously extracted iron from the depths of the lake to the Goth he returned it, and happily returned to the work he had begun. The conversation was satisfied before the rest, and they went down to the sea and entered the boat. would persist at all. Therefore, trusting in the help of Almighty God and the merits of B. Father Benedict, they put the handle on the horse. In a strange way, the iron immediately stuck to the handle, and after pulling it out, they returned to their work rejoicing, thanking God and B. Benedict.

SERMON AT THE COUNCIL OF BENEVENTO

Theophilus, I recall this miracle performed both in the Old Testament by Eliseus, and in the New by the most holy Benedict. But while I consider that the merits of these and those are at a great distance, I confess that I conceive in my mind a greater wonder at this recently accomplished miracle.

Desire This deed, dearest brother, we must not so much impute to them, as to those, in whose merits I trusted, they attempted to do it. Nevertheless, you want me to tell you something about those possessed by the devil, who, with divine mercy, supported the merits of B. Benedict, cared for in this monastery of his, so that the hearts of the hearers may be strengthened more and more in the praises of God, and may be heated manifold in the love of the supreme divinity.

Theophilus Whatever you wish to say for the edification of the audience, go ahead: but I confess that I listen to these things with pleasure.

Desire A certain boy, lying in bed together with his father in the house of a guest, when he had arisen for bodily necessity in the very silence of the night, suddenly a huge lion roaring with its teeth, ready to tear him apart with its claws, appeared to him horrible, who, terrified with terror, cried out, and fell to the ground. At the sound of which the father, troubled at once, arose from bed, hastened to him, and came very anxiously, why he had cried so, or what had become of him, and with the first care he asked anxiously. He reported that he saw a huge lion coming towards him, trembling and trembling. whom the father, having soothed with flattery, took in his own arms, and brought him back to the bed. But the devil, who had appeared to him in the form of a lion, entered into him, and after several days began to torment him most violently. And when he was brought to the church before the altar of the Blessed Benedict, in a strange way, lying prostrate on the floor with his eyes closed, whoever entered the gate of the monastery, immediately uttered his name, saying: Such a man, or such a man, only enters through the gate of the monastery. But a certain brother, having come down from the monastery to the city for the sake of obedience, took twelve denarii from a certain one, and, taking them secretly for the sake of his own advantage, put them into his own pocket. And when he returned to the monastery, and approached the boy in the place where he was tormented, the devil immediately began to slander him in this way through the boy's mouth before his brothers, saying: This monk, contrary to the rule of his order, has taken twelve denarii from such a man for his own advantage, and keeps them hidden in pocket When, therefore, he was asked by his brethren whether the accusations which the old enemy had hurled at him verbally were true, he immediately, crying out his guilt, professed that it was absolutely so.

Another brother also, whose name, lest he suffer embarrassment, I omit, brought from another monastery to ours for the sake of his salvation, one night at the nocturnal vigils, was reciting a lesson from the Old Testament in the church, as usual, to the resident brethren, when perhaps a boy who was being tormented was present. And suddenly the devil, crying out through his mouth, protested that he knew all that was being read, and that he had been there; and adding, he reproved the words of this kind of reader: But if, says he, I were willing to relate before those present what I know of you, I should surely put you to great shame. And indeed that brother was found to have lived in a secular way in his monastery. Therefore, after the brothers had prayed for a long time before the tomb of BP Benedict for the troubled boy, the result was so healthy that he no longer seemed to be troubled by the evil spirit.

At the same time, another boy saw a huge Ethiopian standing on the roof, who, greatly frightened, immediately took flight. But the same demon, pursuing him to the door of the house, prostrated himself on the ground, and immediately entering upon him, severely exhausting the wretch. And when he had been repeatedly brought to the oratory to the tomb of the aforesaid Father for several days, he departed, leaving the demon that had invaded him, by the merits of the same Father, so that he did not dare to approach him any further.

Another certain one, John by name, who still survives at an advanced age, and serves in a home for the sick from the province of Mars, from which he had been born, when he was possessed by the worst demon, this was brought to the convent to recover his salvation by his relatives, who doubtless believed in his merits B. They were blessed to be able to receive salvation, at the threshold of which they had heard that many, occupied with various ailments, had been restored to their former health. And he himself, not long after having expelled the enemy, having recovered his health, brought great joy to those who saw him.

Theodoricus, also a monk and priest, who is still alive and lives with us in this convent, leading a religious life, had a grandson, whom he loved very much in the world; into whom the ancient enemy entered, not, however, to oppress him openly, but secretly bringing on weakness, as if presenting a palsy to those who saw him. And so the aforesaid uncle of his, for the purpose of recovering his health, caused him to be brought to him, trusting in the merits of BP Benedict. But when in this monastery he had continued to be sick for some time as he had been, and no one believed that he was possessed by a demon, one day he was called by his uncle to a venerable man named Lambertus, who was in this nearby forest near the church of the saints and martyrs Cosmas and Damian lived in seclusion, so that they might enjoy their blessing, and he was brought. To whom the man of God gave the blessed bread and commanded him to eat. And when he had put what he had received into his mouth, and had tasted it while eating, the demon, which had hitherto been hidden in him, not being able to bear the blessing of such a gift, by making a noise, shouting, and tossing to and fro, became aware of what was the cause of his languor. But after he had returned to the monastery with his uncle, and it was plainly known that he was possessed by a demon, he was led into the oratory, where all the brethren gathered together to pray to the Almighty Lord for him. Having finished the prayer and psalms, at six o'clock the friars go to the refectory, leaving with him two or three monks, for the purpose of restoring the bodies. Therefore, when those who remained were tearfully praying for divine mercy for him, to the extent that he deigned to free the captive man through the intercession of his most blessed confessor, Benedict, the monk with venerable gray hair appeared to the same person who was being tormented, standing before the altar: who with the ancient power commanded the enemy to withdraw from him. Soon the demon, having made a great attack, came out of the besieged with vomiting, and did not presume to approach him any further. It was discovered that he was undoubtedly the old man B. Maurus, whose remains the brothers who had remained in the church with the same besieged person, had placed on his chest with great devotion and hope. He, however, having been freed from the devil, became a monk, and in this monastery, he continues to serve the rest with his brothers in Jesus Christ our Lord.

A certain peasant dwelt in the neighborhood of this monastery in a castle called Sancti Angeli, who celebrated the festival of Blessed Nicholas the Confessor of Christ every year together with his family as devoutly as he could. On that day, when his sacred solemnity was celebrated by the faithful, he came to the basilica consecrated to his name, with his wife and son, still in his infancy, to offer an offering to the Lord. But after they had finished the solemnities of the mass and had partaken of the communion of the holy body and blood of the Lord, they had returned to their own house, and the boy asked his father for permission to return to the field. Whom the father checked, saying: It is not worthy, O son, to go out into the field to-day to do the work of the field, because, although unworthy, we have received the divine sacraments, and the festival of our patron, namely the most blessed Nicholas, is remembered everywhere with great devotion by all. But he, given up to childish levity, after he was unable to obtain what he had asked of his father, despised his father's orders, secretly flew away from home, and set out alone to visit the countryside. But when, having tarried for some time in the field, he saw that the sun was going down, and that dark night was almost upon the land, he went to a neighboring forest, lest he should be seen to return empty, and by this means he might receive the favor of his father, whose words he had despised, he cut wood, and went home. And when he had already begun to arrange the wood into a package, he suddenly felt a sound coming against him as if a violent spirit; and lifting up his head, he saw a very black bird in the form of a vulture, flying with great speed through the air above him, which met him not far off on the path by which the boy had to return. And so, as he turned towards her, terrified and trembling, she showed herself, transforming herself, into the form of a very black child, whose hair was shaggy and stood up, and the outermost part of his clothes seemed to end in a blush. Therefore, while the boy, fearful as he was, looked with his heart at what he saw, the same ancient enemy addressed him in this way: Make it, O my boy, with all your might, and come with me to the bank of this nearest river; and there I will give you a great supply of gold and silver, so that you may return home laden not with wood, but with gold and silver, so that, while you survive, surpassing all your relatives and neighbors in wealth, you may enjoy a nobler and more delicious life on earth. And this his ancient enemy persuaded him, not so that he might grant what he had promised, but that he might kill him by drowning in the river. But the boy, frequently invoking the name of Christ, endeavored to fortify himself with the sign of the cross; and in a mournful voice he gave such answers: Far be it from me, far be it, that I should ever become the servant of anyone, except that of God Almighty, who created me, and who begat me, my father. When, therefore, he had again and again made the sign of salvation to himself, the demon, who was seen, moving from thence into the neighboring waves of the river, drowned with a great noise, and there began to hiss snakes, bray donkeys, bellow bulls, roar lions, and instilled only fear in the poor fellow. so that the whole forest seemed to him to be spinning in vertigo. And when he was lying almost lifeless on the ground, and completely unaware of what he was doing, behold, suddenly an old man with a mitered head, white, dressed in a robe, appeared to him standing by, and said to him: What are you doing here, when the hour is already dragging on, and as they all retreat, they are already almost alone did they remain in the field? Get up as soon as possible, and return home in haste, lest, if you stay here any longer, you run into serious danger. So, rising from the ground, when he bent down to lift the bundle, the same old man who had been seen disappeared. And behold, once more the evil spirit, entering before his eyes, began to speak to the boy with the same words as before. But he, in spite of what he urged, completely denying what he was going to do, fell to the ground weeping and wailing, and, as he knew and was able, begged the mercy of the Savior of all, Jesus Christ, to provide him with help. Presently the venerable old man, who had appeared to him a little while before, appeared again, and exhorted him to get up quickly, taking away the wood and carrying it away. At whose approach the enemy who seemed to have disappeared like smoke. Of course, we believe that Nicholas was an old man, the blessed Nicholas, whose festival the aforesaid peasant had given his attention to on that day. But the boy rose from the ground at the command of the old man, lifted the bundle, and returned home with great speed, and as he afterwards reported, that bundle of wood became so light to him that it seemed to have no weight. But when he had delayed a little in returning home, the demon that had appeared to him entered into him and began to tire him terribly. Both of them were distraught, the absent parent, and the whole family stood around mourning and crying. But they saw that they could afford him no help, and having found a sound plan, they led him to the threshold of the monastery of the Blessed Benedict, and at his venerable tomb on the right side of the altar, tearfully imploring the mercy of the Lord, prostrated themselves, and there, being besieged, he fell asleep, greatly fatigued. Therefore, while he was lying thus tired and asleep, he suddenly saw an opening from the side, and a man came forward with a very bright appearance and dressed in a white dress and pressing his belly and breast for a long time, ordered him to rise and depart. As soon as he awoke, he got up so well that he no longer felt the demonic infestation upon him. I heard all this in order, from the mouth of the child who had suffered, tearfully relating it.

Theophilus I greatly admire what you tell of what happened to the boy, and I wonder, trembling at the judgments of Almighty God, why he, who with his father was devoutly celebrating the feast of B. Nicholas, and perceived the communion of Dominic's body and blood, allowed him to be freed by an unclean spirit.

Desire If you notice how much it is a crime not to obey your parents, when the Scripture says: Honor your father and your mother, that you may live long upon the earth (Ex. 20:12). And again: It is better to obey than to sacrifice, and to listen rather than to offer the fat of rams, since it is as if it were a sin to resist, to resist; and as the crime of idolatry, do not consent (I Ki. 15:23, 24). And Solomon: Hear, my son, the discipline of your father, and do not forsake the law of your mother, that grace may be added to your head, and tortures to your neck (Prov. 1:8, 9). And in another place: How bad of a reputation is he who leaves his father and is cursed by God who angers his mother (Ecc. 3:18). By the just judgment of God, you will prove that it happened. God therefore allowed this boy to be flogged for his disobedience: but with his usual piety he did not suffer him to remain longer under the same beating, so that everyone may understand from this how much danger disobedience creates, and how humbly he must submit himself to obey his parents.

Theophilus, the words of your answer seem to have satisfied my question.

In the episcopate of Teatini there is a noble monastery near the foot of Mount Majelli, built in honor of the holy Liberator, and subordinate to this our

Casinense convent, where a great multitude of brothers reside, according to the commandment of the blessed Benedict, and serve Christ the Lord and the King as soldiers.

At a certain time, then, while the brothers were resting in the silence of the night in the same monastery according to custom, a certain venerable man appeared to one of them, clothed in a monastic habit, exhorting him to rise quickly from the bed in which he was lying. And when he had risen perniciously to his command, he said to him: Make haste and rouse all the brethren, and that they rise quickly and proceed to the church, insisting with loud cries, because this room, in which they rest, is subject to all haste. And he, obeying the orders, began to cry out in a loud voice: Arise, inquisitive, brothers, rise, and from this cell, for it is about to be destroyed, get out as quickly as possible, lest by tarrying in it any longer, we may overwhelm what is far from the ruins. When, therefore, they awoke, disturbed by his cries, to inquire how he knew these things, he reported in order what he had seen and what had been said to him. Soon therefore the brethren, leaving thence hastily, entered the church, and, as usual, the nocturnal synacis, beating the signs, began to sing to the Lord. And when they had performed their usual duties with intent minds, suddenly the aforesaid house, given a great noise, completely collapsed. Terrified, the brothers went on in haste, anxious lest any of their number should be crushed by that fall, to investigate: and when they were rolling the fallen material hither and thither, they found that one of the brothers, burdened with old age, had remained unharmed under the ruins on all sides, and being drawn outside, they curiously inquired how he had escaped. And he said: When the house, utter ruin, was collapsing upon me, suddenly a splendid man, clothed in monastic garb, stood by me, and the very ruin that was rushing upon me, and threatening to crush me, by supporting me with his arm, kept me safe, as you see. He is indeed believed to have been the blessed Benedict, who, with paternal piety, rescued the flock of Dominic, who were fighting under his mastership, by his admonition and protection, and defended the old man, who was not able to flee, with the hand of his concern.

There was also a certain brother in the same monastery called John, who, pressed by age and infirmity, drew the last breath of his life. When, therefore, one day some of the brethren came to him to sing the morning praises as usual, he rebuked them in as loud a voice as he could, saying: I do not want you to sing the canonical hours for me any longer, because the lord abbot and many of the brethren dressed in white robes came to visit me only as a grace they came, and singing to me the morning service, they said they would come here a little later, and take me with them. While the brothers who had come to him, intent on his vision, and anxiously lamenting whether what he had reported were true, after the space of one hour that brother breathed his last with great joy. From this we can observe that it was Benedictus BP who appeared to him with that sermon of the Albatross, and took him with him, as he had promised. These things which I brought back, I found written in a certain old page in a rather unskilled pen, and I endeavored to associate them with ours now in a little book.

Because the almighty God sometimes shows his miracles not only in great things, but also in the smallest things, so that the faith of believers increases more and more, and the whole creation breaks out in the praises of its Creator, when it is seen that he cares with paternal piety in all things granted to human use. I will not neglect to relate in part what was done about the lamps in this church in our times, as I learned from the venerable monk Gregory, who is still the guardian of the same church.

One day, when one of the guards had lit a lamp in the oratory before the altar, by stirring it with fire, and had raised it up almost to the ceiling, it suddenly slipped and fell on the floor before the altar. God is wonderful in his works! Not only was it not broken, but neither was oil spilled, nor was the fire kindled in it extinguished.

At another time, when the aforesaid Gregory wanted to repair the lamp before the image of the Savior, which was painted above the doors of the church, he found that it hung in the air by extended hooks in such a way that it was supported by no material at all. He immediately summoned the brothers who were standing nearby and showed them that they should be witnesses of such a miracle, which he marveled at.

SERMON AT THE COUNCIL OF BENEVENTO

Moreover, at another time in this same church of the blessed Benedict, on that night which preceded the day on which his festival was held, I received from those who were present at this miracle; while at the vigil one of the watchmen was restoring the lamp before the image of the same blessed Benedict, it suddenly fell to the floor and remained unharmed. I extinguished the fire in it, by the divine preserving power, he was able.

In the oratory of this monastery there are several miracles of this kind wrought by lamps: which, because they are very simple, we have decided to write superfluously. But we have written these things for this reason, lest, because they are small, they should appear to be altogether despised. Now one thing that has slipped from memory in the previous book, to relate in its own order, in which I promised to tell you how Almighty God has often rescued this monastery from the hands of tyrants, we have thought it expedient to write in this second, lest it slip from memory.

While in the time of our predecessor Athenulf the estates of this monastery were fiercely infested by the count of Aquinas, and neither the prayers of the monks, nor the reverence of the alms of the blessed Benedict, who had been the founder and builder of this convent, softened his mind, so that he might restrain himself in some way from the injury of this place, the aforesaid abbot of necessity compelled, after he saw that the ferocious spirit of the man could not be appeased in any way, he brought some of the Northmen, who at that time were coming to Italy in the hire of our princes, into the possessions of this monastery, in so far as he could protect them from the aforesaid count through them. After they had received houses in which to stay, and the wages with which they were supported, they began to defend all that belonged to the monastery, after the manner of active soldiers, nobly and faithfully defending the enemies around them. Therefore, when the aforesaid abbot, and who had succeeded him in the government in the second degree, survived, the hired soldiers remained quite honestly in their fidelity; , he gradually began to be unfaithful and hostile to us; which, like a dog and a serpent, roll every day to our destruction, taking away from us one way or the other, in the lust of the sacrilegious leadership of their own right. Wherefore it came to pass that, from such and such a large possession, nothing else was left to our advantage, except the city, which is situated at the foot of the mountain of Casin, with the farms of four or five villages; , taking away their wealth, they gave us misery and want. When, therefore, for a considerable period of time they had been doing this incessantly without any piety of heart, and the merciful and pious Lord had decided to help his servants who were suffering from hunger and poverty, with his kindness, the most blessed Benedictus appeared in a vision to a certain peasant living in the village of a certain village of ours, and as going out, he ordered them to follow him. And when the same peasant turned his attention to the same vision, it seemed to him that the most blessed Benedictus, with the rod which he carried in his hand, would expel all the Northmen, who had invaded his possessions, from the ends of this earth by mighty power, and eliminate them from the inheritance of the monastery, empty of possessions and burdened with ignominy. In the same year, therefore, the aforesaid Norman band, more than usual by their audacity, to our calamity, took possession of the citadel which is called St. Andrew's, in order that they might be able to keep it more safely taken from us; After they had taken possession of the same citadel, they gathered together one day and entered with great pride the aforesaid city of Casin. Therefore, the inhabitants of this land, united in a flock, and assisted by their neighbors on every side, set their minds on the siege of the same fortress. (I am going to say wonderful) the siege was made, while the arrows were fired from both sides with a sharp thrust, the cannon of the Normans, as if twisted by the breath of the wind, smote those by whom they had been sent. What is the need of many? when they saw that they were thus attacked by themselves, and were no longer able to resist any longer, seeing that it was difficult for them to kick against the spur (and that they knew that the divine right hand was fighting against them), they surrendered themselves into the hands of the abbot and monks; they were staying in the town of Aversano, they were released. And so it came to pass that from that time, by the merits of the blessed Benedict, this land in which we dwell remains unharmed from their infestation and remains secure under the protection of that saint.

The mode of this book compels us to strive to the end. But the good of obedience, which is the first among the other virtues, does not allow us to pass over in utter silence the virtue of a certain brother, who followed it with all humility of heart even unto death: namely, imitating him, who became obedient to the Father unto death (Phil. 2). He left us an example of obedience as well as of patience.

SERMON AT THE COUNCIL OF BENEVENTO

A brother of this congregation of ours named Raynerius, indeed, was young in age, but old in character: to whom many of the brethren who still survive, and who know him well, testify that he was of such humility and obedience, that he was regarded as wonderful by all.

When one day he was enjoined by his abbot to go to the territory of Theatinus, in order to carry out some work for the benefit of the monastery, he set out joyfully, as always, ready to obey, and hastening to fulfill his orders. While he was proceeding and had already covered a considerable distance of the journey, he was killed by the robbers of a certain powerful man of Oderisius, who, by his order, if they could plunder anything from the things of this monastery, watched the way, and took away all that he was carrying, he was killed. Whose body, either because of the intrigues of his enemies, or because it was far away, could not be brought to this convent, but was delivered to the ground in a certain church nearby. But inasmuch as his obedience to Almighty God was accepted, he deigned to show his extinct body. Many, therefore, seized with sickness, began to hasten to his tomb, and having recovered health, returned safely to their own places. Among whom Count Atto, the son of the great Count Atton, son-in-law of the aforesaid Oderisius, when he was seriously ill with a fever, he came to his tomb, bearing a report, and there, prostrated in prayer, the fever having subsided, he rose up so well that the ill health from which he had previously suffered, nothing he would feel it entirely within himself; who, giving thanks for his recovered health, departed rejoicing in recompense for so great a service, with the best mantle offered over his tomb.

And since we began to mention the wonders of God, which happened to me myself, I did not allow him to pass by in silence, saying that the Scripture says that it is good to hide the secret of a king, but it is honorable to manifest and reveal the works of God (Tob. 12). When, within the years of my childhood, I was afflicted with a fever, John of blessed memory, a priest of venerable dignity, who was then esteemed famous in the service of God in our city of Beneventan, came hastening to me for the grace of a visitation. And when he had sat down a little with the rest who had come, and beheld me more violently pressed by the Tertian type, moved by the charity which he had towards me, he arose, and with tears pouring out of his mouth, invoking the Lord with a loud voice, laid his hand on my head, and the fever, which attacked me more acutely, soon escaped. He departed.

I will take care to write it at the foot of this pamphlet, which I learned by reference to Leo, the abbot of the monastery of St. Paul the Apostle, who was appointed a second mile from the city of Rome, where his most sacred body was venerated and worshiped shining with signs and wonders. For he said that the most venerable Adam, the very monk and guardian of the church of our monastery, had reported to him that one day, while the same venerable Adam was going out the gate of the monastery to do some work, two young men in the habit of monks met him at the very entrance of the monastery. he inquired, he heard from them that one of them was called Protus, and the other Hyacinthus. But he, astonished as to why they had come, when asked why they had come, said to them: We have come to visit the brothers, who today remember our memory with a devout mind. For it was that day in which, with the blood shed for Christ, they earned the palm of martyrdom by giving it themselves. When, therefore, he had halted a little in astonishment, and they had begun their journey and entered the monastery, he returned to himself, desiring to know more certainly what he had heard, and pursued them at a rapid pace. And while he was diligently searching for them here and there through the monastery, and could not at all find them, and those who met him, he began to ask where the monks were who had just entered the monastery while talking with him. But they professed to have heard of no one entering the monastery but him. In this matter it is clearly given to be understood that those who had appeared to him were truly the holy martyrs Protus and Hyacinth, whose festival was celebrated on that day. I perceived that all these things had been done in the same order by Firmus, a veteran monk of this monastery, namely the nephew of Ada himself, whom he had told me had been placed in Rome, on his return to the monastery.

Let this be the end of this day's prayer: inasmuch as this book having been concluded in honor of so many martyrs, refreshed in mind during the space of this night, we come to the rest of the Acts of the saints, aided by their prayers and those of all the saints, faithfully narrating.

THE THIRD BOOK. Which is about miracles done elsewhere. Having finished the two, accompanied by the grace of Christ, the little books which we have written about the miracles of God, either in this convent or in the cells subject to him, by himself giving generously, we come to the narrative of the third one, granting to the Lord. And since the rest of the things which were done outside the walls of this monastery, and which we perceived by sight or hearing, still remain to be written in the other two pamphlets, it seems to me worthwhile to begin with the head of the Church himself, and so afterwards to come to the individual members in a series of writings.

While, therefore, the negligence of the priests gradually undermined Italy from the right path of religion, it grew into such an evil custom that, after the authority of the sacred law, all things divine and human were mixed up, so that the people chose the election, and the priests the consecration, and the gift of the Holy Spirit, which was freely given and received by the divine authority. had been given and received by hand, led by money, they would have sold it; thus, it would be scarcely possible to find those who, not repulsed by the contagion of this Simoniac pestilence, would exist in the world before God observing the precepts of the Sunday. And so, when the multitude of clerics were treading the path of unbridled license, with no one stopping them, the priests and deacons themselves (who had to treat the Sunday sacraments handed down to them with a clean heart and chaste body) began to marry wives after the manner of the laity, and to leave their adopted children heirs by will; some of the bishops even despised the shame of all, to dwell together in one house with their wives. And this worst and most blasphemous custom flourished most within the city, whence once the rule of religion had spread everywhere by the apostle Peter himself and his successors.

Therefore, while for several years some had obtained the pontifical chair by name alone, a certain Benedict by name, but not by work, the son of a certain consul of Albani (following in the footsteps of Simon Magus rather than Simon Peter), with no small amount of money lavished on the people, claimed the highest priesthood for himself; indeed, after attaining the priesthood, I am horrified to report how vile, how disgusting, and how blasphemous the life was; rather, how Almighty God was designed to look into the face of the Church, I begin to tell. Finally, when he had been committing robberies, murders, and

SERMON AT THE COUNCIL OF BENEVENTO

other crimes against the Roman people for a considerable period of time, without any delay, the people gathered together, because they could no longer bear his wickedness, and ousted him from the seat of the pontificate, and drove him out of the city; and another in his place, that is to say John the Sabine bishop (not, however, with an empty hand), they substitute the trivial canonical decrees; who for no more than three months used the succession of the Roman chair, Benedictus and his relatives attacking the city from all sides; because he had risen from among the consuls of the land, and among them the greatest virtue, having been beaten with dishonor by the city, he returned to his episcopate. Benedict therefore recovered the priesthood which he had lost, yet he did not in the least change his former manners, according to what is written: Adolescent according to his way; even when he is old, he will not depart from her (Prov. 22). And because it is hard to meditate on the new in the heart of the old, he persevered in the same wicked and perverted works as before. And when he saw himself despised both by the clergy and the people on account of his iniquities, and saw that the ears of all were filled with the report of his exploits, at last he discovered a plan (for, given to pleasure, he preferred to live as Epicurus rather than as a pontiff) to a certain archpresbyter John, who was then more religious than the rest in the city It seemed to the clergy that, having received from him not a small sum of money, he left the high priesthood and gave it up; but he himself, receiving himself in his own castles, gave way to the city. Meanwhile, John, who was given the name Gregory, had administered the priesthood for two years and eight months, when King Henry, who then ruled Germany, Pannonia, Saxony, and Italy, entered Italy to receive from the hand of the Roman Pontiff the imperial crown, in so far as he might henceforth be called Augustus. He went to the Roman city (in 1047). But before he entered the city, a council of many of the bishops, not only the abbot, but also the clergy and religious monks, assembled in the southern city, John, who was called Gregory, was sent to him by the bishops, as concerning ecclesiastical affairs, and especially concerning the Roman Church at that time, which were three together He seemed to have the pontiffs, he himself presiding, to be treated, he asked to come. But these things were done on purpose, for for some time the king had already made up his mind to justly expel those three who had unjustly invaded the apostolic see, with the advice and authority of the whole council, and one who, according to the statutes of St. Dominic was to carefully preside over the flock, choosing the clergy and the people, and was to be ordained. The aforesaid pontiff, having been exhorted by the king and the other pontiffs, went to Sutrium, where the synod was assembled, and attracted by the hope that, after the other two had been deposed, the pontificate alone would be confirmed to him, he went gratefully. But when it had come to that, and the matter had begun to be agitated and discussed by the Synod, recognizing that he was unable to administer the just honor of such a priesthood, he jumped from the pontifical chair, and stripping himself of his pontifical garments, demanded pardon, and abdicated the dignity of the high priesthood.

After these things the king entered the city, assembled in the church of B. Peter the Apostle, the Roman clergy and people, together with the bishops who had assembled in the aforesaid synod, by common counsel they chose Clement of Bamberg as bishop, because there was not then found in the Roman Church such a person as could be worthy of such an honor sufficient for the priesthood: and enthroning him in the apostolic seat to govern the flock of Dominicus. When he had served as a priest not more than nine months, he passed away from this life. Leo succeeded him, of whom we have a discourse beforehand, a man in all things apostolic, of royal birth, endowed with wisdom, prominent in religion, eminently learned in all ecclesiastical doctrine, and who (as it is written) began to invoke the name of the Lord; whom I also saw, and deserved to have his familiarity: many times even with him celebrating mass in the church, I stood with him at the divine altar dressed in sacred clothes, and read the Gospel to him. By which all ecclesiastical studies were renewed and restored, and a new light was seen to arise in the world.

Here he frequently invoked the priestly counsel, removed priests, deacons, and the rest of the clergy not regularly ordained, and appointed in their places those who could serve worthily for the worship of the true and supreme God. Every day also by himself and his disciples sent everywhere, he showed the people the way of the Lord, preaching in letters and words. He who always walked along the apostolic path, also imitated the apostolic men in miracles. Of whom indeed I happened to hear more, but being busy with many affairs, and not being able to run through each and every one, I will endeavor to relate a few of the several, so that by these, whoever reads in future may recognize how much merit this man has had.

Therefore, I learned from Pope Gregory, who was brought up by him and ordained a subdeacon, but now holds the apostolic summit in the city of Rome, who illustrates the Church of Christ with words and examples at the same time, by the relation which I am telling. In whose words I must certainly believe as if I had been present and seen with my own eyes. At one time, while the aforesaid venerable pontiff Leo was staying in Gaul, intent on ecclesiastical affairs, he accepted a wooden cup offered for blessing by the abbot of a certain monastery, the holy confessor of Christ Remigius; which indeed, because of his great love for the pontiff, he was very fond of him, and at the hour of his repast he was accustomed to drink while sitting at table, set on gold and silver plates. One day, as the waiter was sitting at table, as usual, he wanted to hold out a cup, which, through the carelessness of the holder, it fell from his hand, and soon it was broken into pieces. Finally, when the most blessed pope twice or thrice required wine, and the waiter delayed coming for this reason, he was told that the cup in which he was accustomed to drink had fallen from his hand, and had been broken; When he heard this, he was greatly saddened, not so much because of the loss of the cup, as because, having received the vessel from the monastery of St. Remigius, for the sake of the blessing, he saw himself frustrated. And when it had been brought to him, seeing both broken, he implored the Almighty Lord that by the merits of B. Remigius he might restore to him the broken cup, which he loved so dearly for his love. And soon he joined the other part to the other, so that at the same moment it was solidified so that no trace of what had been broken remained, all who were present marveling and applauding in his veneration. He began to impute this not to his own, but to the merits of B. Remigius, from whose monastery, by the grace of charity, he had received that office.

Theophilus, In this miracle of both of them, or of the other, that of Benedictus, though of a different subject, I likewise hear, that the first miracle was to be renewed, while he rejoined the camp divided into parts. (*Greg. book II, Dialog.*)

In the meantime, my dearest brother, you must be silent, inasmuch as you are intent on knowing these greater things about him. At another time, therefore, (as the aforesaid pope Gregory reported to me), a certain bishop of Gaul had been suspended by the same pontiff Leo in the honor of a bishop; a certain priest of which, named Gibert, eloquent in speech and not moderately learned in letters, had promised the same bishop that he would come to Rome, and by his clever assertions deceive the same blessed pontiff, and obtain the restoration of the office which had been taken from him: and so, receiving money from him, he came to Rome. And when he had presented himself to the most blessed pontiff, he began to turn hither and thither like a cunning serpent, to excuse his bishop with rhetorical words, with flattering and humble prayers, that the forbidden office, unjustly taken away, as he claimed, should be restored, and lamented. But when what he asked for had been denied him, and he could not deceive him as he had hoped, lest it should be seen that he should return to his bishop, from whom he had received not a little money, without effect, he sought another resource. furtive letters, and sealed with the apostolic seal, to be delivered to his bishop, which signified both the episcopal office and the grace of the apostolic see rendered to him. This fact did not hide the blessed Leo in the least, and immediately calling the aforesaid priest, taking the money he had offered, and putting it into his hand, he said: Let your money be with you in perdition, because you have secretly tried to possess the gift of God with money (Acts 8). Whose speech was soon followed by divine vengeance, so that from that day to this day he wandered everywhere in a lost mind, and no house or prison could hold him longer than two or three days.

In this matter it is clearly understood that anyone who has attempted to deceive or to provoke to anger one who lives in the just by a reckless venture has without a doubt offended the Lord.

Theophilus, It is so as you say, but I beseech you, if you still meet with the spirit of the virtue of such a great Father, continue unsparingly.

While the most blessed pontiff Leo had for five years piously and most religiously administered the priesthood granted to him by God, he migrated from this unstable light to Christ, who is the true and eternal light, with the rejoicing citizens of heaven, supported by angelic hands. And indeed, paradise was open to him when he received the company of the saints. But the unfortunate world, which did not deserve to have such a pontiff for a long time. After his death many and great miracles were performed by the Lord at his tomb and in other places through him. Of which I have left out only two others (because I hasten to recount the deeds of others), for the sake of edification I have appended to this book.

Pope Victor, who had succeeded him in the priestly reign (as has been related to us by truthful men), having heard the report of his miracles, that the Lord would work such things through him, did not accommodate his faith. But because, as the Apostle says: Tongues are a sign not to the faithful but to the unbelieving (1 Cor. 14), the Almighty Lord wanted to teach him by an experiment which, having been heard by many, he did not at all want to believe.

A certain bishop of Curia, whose name has been lost from memory, coming from Germany with the aforesaid pontiff Victor, stayed in his service at Rome; he had a child mute from his mother's womb, whom he used to take with him wherever he went, feeding and clothing him as a reward for his soul, and in whose empty mouth there seemed not even a trace of language. Even the bishop who performed the miracles at the tomb of B. Leo, in the same way as the pope, had an unbelieving attitude. When, therefore, one day he had decided to return to the seat of his episcopate, having already received permission, he entered the church of blessed Peter the Apostle, after having commended himself more attentively to his clients, mounted on horses, and forgetting the boy in the same church, hastened the way that led him to He was leading his country, leaving the city, marching. When, therefore, he was still a long way from the city, he suddenly remembered that he had left a mute child in the church of blessed Peter. He soon stopped, and dismissed some of his servants, from whom the child was to be brought back. Therefore, when they had entered the basilica of the prince of the apostles, they saw a boy standing before the tomb of the blessed Leo and talking with those who stood around. To those wondering and asking how this had happened to him, the boy said: After my master departed, leaving me here in the church, I betook myself hither to the tomb of blessed Leo, if by chance the almighty Lord would deign to restore to me the office which I lacked, by the merits of his voice. Nor was I cheated of my vow, which I desired in my heart, but as soon as I lay prostrate for a little while weeping before his venerable memory, I immediately rose up, speaking with a recovered voice, as you yourselves see. And from that day, and what is more wonderful, the tongue which had been missing began to grow in his mouth little by little, so that within a few days he received his tongue completely in his mouth, and uttered words without hindrance. Finally, those who had been sent took care to bring the boy to the bishop, and whom he had left silent, they brought him to speak to him in support of the merits of the blessed Leo. The bishop therefore returned to the Roman pontiff, and showed what the Almighty Lord had deigned to do through blessed Leo. From that time, they themselves began to preach his venerable merits to all, which they did not suffer others to hear before reporting.

Theophilus, They are liked because they are wonderful, but more because they are new.

The illustrious man Maximus, a citizen of the city of Rome, recently reported to me about the same venerable prince whom I am telling. Bernardus was a certain soldier of the worst mind, who showed himself contrary to the apostolic see in every way he could. But in the war which was committed by the neighbors who remained around the city, conspiring with Cadalus, bishop of Parma, who was then attempting to invade the apostolic see, with the soldiers who were defending the Roman Church, he was stabbed to death by the just judgment of God. Here, then, having heard the report of the miracles which Almighty God had shown to the faithful people through the merits of the blessed Leo, he not only did not believe, but also mocked and blasphemed with his sacrilegious mouth. Finally, when he appeared one day in the assembly of the people, and a discussion had arisen among them about the signs and virtues of the blessed Leo, he began to laugh, saying: If he is holy, as you say, let him pinch my finger, and let those who stood by check him, lest such things should be said of a holy man. to speak, he dismissed the meeting and left. When, by chance, the dog that was following him attacked his dog in the street. But he, lest the pig should be torn to pieces, ran hastily, and with his thrusting hand he wished to hold the dog; but soon the pig with its gaping mouth bit his finger, so that from that day all the time that he lived his finger was contracted, he could not stretch it in any way. Wherefore it came to pass that he who had presumed to mock the servant of God, himself, with a contracted finger, was held to be laughed at by all. These things which have been said about Father B. Leo are sufficient, so that, since we are hastening to recount the deeds of others, we will leave others, who have leisure, to write the many more wonderful things that are said about him.

What the Lord says in the Gospel: My Father still works, and I work (John 5:17), we see every day being fulfilled, and ancient miracles renewed in new times. These things, therefore, which I am about to say, are so clear, that it is evident that Rome is well known, not only in the diocese of Florence, where the facts are known, but also in the whole of Tuscany, and in the city which is the capital of the world.

Peter is a certain cleric, who secretly received the episcopal seat in the aforesaid city of Florence, with the support of the kingdom. Finally, when he had been kindly received by the clergy and the people, as befits a bishop, after not much time the rumor spread through the diocese of the same episcopate that, disgusted by the plague of the Simoniac heresy, which it was ordained to receive and give freely, by the commandment of the Lord, he had bought money. And when so horrible and so blasphemous a report had first reached the religious, and afterwards the ears of the common people, many began to withdraw from his communion. Who, having assembled the counsel of the bishops, summoned the same bishop, that he might carefully acknowledge the matter. But when he had presented himself to the synod, the accusers being hailed from all sides, he endeavored to purify himself by the sacrament. And when the matter had been a little agitated before those present, inferences were given, that, perhaps induced by them, he might humbly confess, fearing the divine judgment which he obstinately denied, inasmuch as he would not be removed from eternity to the altar, if he had abstained from this present, whom he could not justly minister to. In the meantime, the people were divided into two parties, of which the other, which preferred the love of God to the gifts, the clerics and religious monks, who had undertaken to prove the matter against the bishop; the other, who loved gifts and favors, followed the bishop. When, therefore, the people often quarreled with each other, and one side opposed the other, the contention arose to such an extent that, when they fought with each other, they often even came to the point of shedding blood. And when these things were going on longer, and neither side yielded to the other, the most reverend John, abbot of the monastery called Umbrosa Vallis, often an advocate for this conflict, led by the zeal of God, came with his monks, who, exhorting, preaching, intending the examination of the divine judgment, did not cease to admonish the bishop as far as he would do penance for the fault he had committed, and he would humbly yield to the priesthood, which was at

SERMON AT THE COUNCIL OF BENEVENTO

least legally acquired, and would not be to the detriment of himself and his subjects, to whom he ought to have increased. Repeatedly proposing to him that of the Gospel, how the Lord Jesus threw those selling and buying doves from the temple, overturned the chairs, and poured out the money-changers' money (John 2:15), in other words showing that whoever receives the gift of the Holy Spirit, which is signified by the dove, is led by greed, or lifted up in vain glory, and having tried to buy or sell at a price, he knew beyond a doubt that he would be eliminated from that heavenly temple and eternal altar. But he, nevertheless, desirous of the honor of his present life, led the holy man's counsels to nothing, nay, on the contrary, he persistently endeavored to defend himself with arms and words, and with all the means he could. And when the same venerable abbot saw that his words were unsuccessful, both sides of the people advocated: Since, he said, words are of no avail, let us come to signs. Let a pyre be built, and lighted with a supposed fire, through which one of our number may enter, that it may be proved whether what we say of the bishop is true or false, the Lord discerning. The opinion is pleasing to both parties: the pile is soon built to measure twelve feet; within which a small path is left, through which the person of one man only could pass: which is also made of kindled wood, lest there should be any space left vacant by the flame. In the meantime, while these things were being prepared, the aforesaid abbot John instructed his disciple Peter, the most reverend, a man who was afterwards ordained bishop in the city of Albany, and who still remains governing the same church, to offer a sacrifice to Almighty God dressed in sacred clothes. And thus, at last, confident of God's mercy, he would undoubtedly enter through the flames of the burning stake.

He who, obeying the commandments of the Father, after having offered sacrifice to God, stripped himself of his hut, came to the fire, and with a loud voice: I pray, says he, almighty God, if Peter, who is called a bishop, is the foul pestilence of Simonia, let not your Church be polluted any more, by the judgment of St. Show me the strength of your spirit: grant me to pass through this fire unharmed. But if we, being full of delusions, led by reason of envy, have taken this question against him, let the ardor of this fire consume me, forsaken by your grace. Saying these things and securing himself with the seal of the holy cross, he steadily entered through the midst of the flames. When, therefore, he was surrounded by flames on every side, so that no one could see him at all, and everyone thought that he was already consumed, he suddenly sprang out from another side, accompanied by the grace of Christ, so that not only his clothes, but not even a hair was seen to be injured by the fire. . But, as the same venerable man later reported, when he was walking through the midst of the flames, the map fell from his hand. And when he was about to come out of the fire, he saw that he was not carrying the bag in his hands, and, considering that it had fallen into the fire, he returned again through the flames, and taking out the bag with him, he brought it back. Then all who were present, having seen so great and so astonishing a miracle, gave immense thanks to God, and soon the different parties were united, and drove the aforesaid bishop out of the church.

Theophilus, I wonder with joy, and I rejoice with wonder, that in the time of our mediocrity I look upon that ancient and glorious miracle of the three boys, when they came out of the burning fireplace whole and uncorrupted with their whole bodies.

The venerable pope Gregory, whose memory I have mentioned above, is often accustomed to report to me what the heresy against the same Simoniac, when the Lord wanted to show himself in his presence. When, he says, I was a subdeacon, and had been sent by Victor of blessed memory, the pontiff of this apostolic see to Gaul to discuss ecclesiastical affairs, it was my concern to convene a council of bishops, that we might deal with ecclesiastical affairs before them. In the same city in which the synod was held, there was a bishop who was slandered by many as having acquired the honor of the episcopate at a price. So, the bishop was called and came to the middle. When, therefore, we began to exhort him with salutary admonitions, that he should be opposed to everything, his conscience already confessing, he humbly confessed, both because he was the bishop of the same city, and also because he relied on the help of the count of his own land, full of pride he utterly despised our words. But when, by us and the rest of the bishops who were present, he saw that he was constrained under the rule of justice, which he had not hoped for, and that he had no leave to escape, he began to obstinately deny what he had scarcely deigned to hear before. And when the words were produced at length, and the greatest part of the day had been spent, and the man nevertheless persisted in his obstinacy in denying, it was thought to swear to us with the rest of the religious bishops who were present, and to commit the whole judgment in the manifestation of the Holy Spirit. In the name, I say, of the Father, and of the Son, and of the Holy Spirit, whose gift of grace we have heard that you have procured, that we may swear that you have told us the truth of this matter. But if, as you have begun, you try to deny the Holy Spirit, until you confess what is true, you will not be able to name it. That bishop, when he was eloquent and was exhorted by us to name the Holy Spirit, indeed named the Father and the Son quite eloquently, but he could not in any way strangely name the Holy Spirit. Then it became more clearly evident to all who were present that he had bought the honor of the episcopate with a given price, which is given only by the generous grace of the Holy Spirit. Then the bishop, shaken by the power of the Holy Spirit, was forced humbly to confess before all that which before, inflated with the pride of God, he had presumptuously denied after fear.

Theophilus Since the Father, the Son, and the Holy Spirit are one, and it is right to feel nothing else about the Father and the Son than about the Holy Spirit, why is it that in uttering the words of the Father and the Son, the language is loose and eloquent, but in the name of the Holy Spirit alone, as it were, the tongue is mute and did he have a tie at all?

Desire By the just judgment of God, it happened that he who bought the gift of the Holy Spirit of grace, which is both freely given and received, with a pleading tongue, did not have the special duty of the tongue in uttering the word of the Holy Spirit.

Alferius was abbot of the monastery of the Holy Trinity, built by him on the side of the mountain, which overlooks the sea between the cities of Salernitana and Amalfitana: whose religious and God-loving life I personally saw, who stayed with him for some time familiarly, and recognized from other references. But the miracle which the divine power deigned to work in him, and which I have learned from many, it is right not to pass over in silence. Finally, while he was going to the city of Salernitana for the benefit of the monastery, he was walking along the path of a precipitous mountain and fell down with the horse on which he was sitting over an immense precipice, which lies at such a height above the sea, that it seems to be fifty or more paces high. So while those who went with him doubtless thought that he was extinct, they were very sad and weeping, and took care to go down by a certain inlet to the sea, if at least they could somehow find him so that they could deliver him to the burial. And when, under the foot of the mountain, treading on the soft sands near the shore of the sea, they hastened to the place where he had fallen, they found him on the road safe and sound, mounted on the horse on which he had fallen, and hastily begun his journey to Salerno. And when they were astonished and could not at all judge how things had come to pass, they began to give thanks to God, and raised their voices as if in tumult. But suddenly pressed by him, they hear the precept: If, says he, you wish to enjoy my blessings, you shall not dedicate to anyone, as long as I live, what you have seen from me.

It is also said of him that he raised the dead, which, indeed, to those who know him and his life intimately, does not seem at all incredible.

Leo the abbot, who succeeded him in the government of the monastery, having brought him up under his mastership, holding the office of superior in obedience, who was more closely attached to him than the rest of the brothers, recently reported to me that at one time secular men came to him as a visitation, in order to enjoy his prayers. Desiring to provide them with a spiritual as well as a corporal refreshment, he ordered the aforesaid Leo, his superior, for the sake of charity, to set a table for them and prepare a meal. He replied that he had nothing but bread and wine and five chicken eggs that he could provide for them to eat; but how the eggs themselves were to be divided among them, I do not know: there were certainly seven of them. To whom he said: Make haste, as much as possible, and prepare the same eggs with fire, and bring them to me to set them. He ran and, as he had been ordered, boiled the eggs, and brought them to him as he had ordered. When he received it, he blessed it, and from the five sheep, he gave one to each of the seven men, which is a wonderful thing.

Theophilus When I consider the five eggs distributed among seven people to be increased in this way, so that each one receives an equal lot, I see it in a way a miracle, by which the Author of all five loaves satisfied five thousand people (Matt. 16:9).

SERMON AT THE COUNCIL OF BENEVENTO

Desire My father's aunt, Bella by name, lived in the monastery of Blessed Peter the Apostle within the city of Benevento, in a saintly habit from the prime of her youth to her final old age. When she was betrothed to a man, she fled secretly from her parents' house and made her way to a monastery, where she dedicated her virginity to the Lord Almighty; and, because he scorned to have an earthly spouse on earth, he undoubtedly deserved to have a heavenly one in the heavens. She used to tell me about her abbess, who was called Offa. She lived for a long time on the mountain, which is called St, Agatha the Martyr, near the city of Capuan, before she assumed the government of the monastery, and led a hermit life there. When, therefore, he wanted to throw the incense into the furnace, it fell from his hand, and the lamp being extinguished by the wind, he was unable to find the incense. But suddenly a certain one stood near him, and taking his hand, gave him the incense which he had placed on the censer. So great an odor emanated from that burnt incense, that throughout the rest of the night, until the third hour of the day, not only the church, but also the whole monastery was filled with a wonderful sweetness. From which fact it is undoubtedly given to be understood that it was the angel of the Lord who gave that incense of such a fragrant odor.

This same most pious abbess, while she had carefully presided over the virgins for many ages, never ceasing to instruct the servants of God entrusted to her with words and examples, was overcome by bodily infirmity and died. And when she was at the end, she was almost ready to give up her life to Christ, whom she had served, when, in the sight of all who were present, she raised herself from her bed as if to the measure of three cubits in the air and stood with her hands outstretched to heaven. And having finished his prayer, placing himself again on the bed, he breathed his last. But from this it may be judged how much abstinence there was. While she was lying sick in bed, and by many respectable men and women who came to her as a visitation, in order to take a little food with which to support her weak body, she was begged, unaccustomed to delicacies; I shall be able to taste a little of it. Oh, the abstinence to be preached in a woman, who, in her infirmity, used infused vegetables for even the highest delicacies! When she had died, and was buried in the church, one day a certain peasant, passing through the same church laden with corn, over her grave, despising the merit of what lay buried there, laid down a sack of corn, and, tired, sat down beside it in order to rest a little.

Suddenly, therefore, the bag was taken up by God from the same tomb and thrown far away, and all the corn that was full of it was scattered here and there throughout the same church. The peasant, therefore, greatly crushed, learned from that day how much the men of God are to be worshiped in the body; when their bodies were extinguished and placed in the sepulcher, lest they should be looked down upon by some, he wished to demonstrate his divine virtue.

Another noble man from the same city of Benevento had come to the monastery for some unknown reason, and perhaps he had sat down over his tomb, when suddenly he was overcome with so much pain in his bowels that, shouting and howling, he thought he would die at that very hour. At whose voice the virgins who were in the monastery immediately ran and told him whose tomb he was sitting on. He who, for ignorance demanded forgiveness, earned medicine by the merits of God's servant in heaven.

In the same city there is a monastery called St. Sophia, subordinate to this monastery of Casin, in which there was a certain monk of holy behavior and great humility from his childhood, who was led to extremes by being prevented by excessive tantrums during the years of his youth. At the end of which the assembled brethren began, with hymns and psalms, to commend his soul to God, and to invoke the congregation of the saints more attentively to his aid: who died of growing infirmity. But while water was being prepared to wash his body, he lay lifeless for about an hour. And when those who were present began to pray and sing psalms, suddenly his whole body trembled, and gradually he revived and sat down on his bed, to the astonishment of all. Then, being questioned, he began to report to them that he had seen coming out of the body, saying: When my soul, singing litanies to you and invoking the saints of the Lord, was going out of the body, immediately at your prayers the saints whom you invoked came to my aid. And what would they require from him if he had been able to recognize those whom he had never seen? He answered: I knew St. Benedict and St. Gregory, I saw B. Donatus and Felix, with the rest of the saints who rest in this church, come to my aid. Among whom our blessed Mercury, our patron, was seen shining like a splendid star. When they asked him whether he was going to stay in this life? "No," said he, "for blessed Mercurius promises to come to-day to take charge of me." What he had said was true, he confirmed the outcome of the matter. For on the same day, when he was withdrawn from this light, he was undoubtedly received by those whom he had previously seen coming to his aid when he was dying. Finally, being placed in the same monastery, I saw one of those who had been present as witnesses, named Sicenolf, surviving, who professed to have seen and heard all these things as said.

LATIN TEXT

Concio habita in synodo Beneventana

Novit vestra dilectio, charissimi fratres coepiscopi (neque latet orbem universum), sancta Romana et apostolica sedes, cui Deo auctore deservio, quot adversa pertulerit, quot denique per Simoniacae haereseos trapezitas malleis tunsionibusque perfracta sit, adeo ut columna Dei vivi videretur jam pene concussa nutare, et sagena summi piscatoris intumescentibus fluctibus disrumpi, ac naufragii sorte perire. Guibertus enim haeresiarcha, qui, vivente sanctae memoriae praedecessore meo Gregorio papa, Romanam invasit Ecclesiam, Antichristi praecursor et Satanae signifer, oves Christi dispergere, mactare laniareque non desinit.

Incitator enim incentorque malorum factus, quantas Gregorio papae injurias, quas persecutiones, quot clades intulerit, referre quis possit? Excitavit contra eum conjuratos ipse conspirationis auctor; fugavit Urbe; sacerdotio, quantum in se fuit, Simoniacus perjurusque primavit, commovit adversus eum Romanum imperium, concitavit gentes et regna; et (quod a seculo est inauditum) excommunicatus ipse atque damnatus sanctum pontificem excommunicare praesumpsit, Romanam urbem hactenus sacrilegiis, caedibus, perjuriis, conspirationibus, flagitiis et vitiorum omnium ludibriis profanare non desinit, et Simonis Magi perfidia incensus, nequitiae suae complices ad tam impium et exsecrabile facinus evocans, coacto imperatoris exercitu, apostolicae sedis invasor effectus est contra praecepta evangelica, contra prophetarum apostolorumque decreta, contra canonum et Romanorum pontificum jura, nullo cardinalium episcoporum praecedente judicio, nullo Romani cleri approbante suffragio, nullo devoti populi requisito consensu in sancta Romana Ecclesia totius nequitiae ac perditionis caput effectus est. Sed omnipotentis Dei potentia cum jam dictum Gregorium pontificem post labores ac certamina plurima ad aeternam requiem evocasset, et unanimi concordia episcopi et cardinales provincialesque antistites una cum Romano clero et populo parvitatem nostram modis omnibus contradicentem et renitentem apostolicae sedi praefecissent, non timens aeterni imperatoris judicium, nunc usque Christum et oves ejus, pro quibus ille fudit sanguinem suum, persequi non omittit. Idcirco auctoritate Dei et beatorum apostolorum Petri et Pauli, omniumque sanctorum, omni illum sacerdotali officio et honore privamus, et, a liminibus Ecclesiae separantes, anathematis vinculo innodamus.

Nostis praeterea et bene nostis quos dolos machinati, sint, quantasque mihi pressuras intulerint Hugo Lugdunensis archiepiscopus, et Richardus Massiliensis abbas, qui pro fastu et ambitione sedis apostolicae, ad quam dudum clam inhiabant, ubi votis suis potiti non sunt, schismata in sancta Ecclesia fecerunt, et Richardus quidem Romae nostram electionem cum cardinalibus et episcopis egerat: Hugo autem ad nos post paululum veniens affusus vestigiis, dum obsequium nobis summo pontifici debitum invitis ac retractantibus exhiberet, legationem a nobis in partibus Galliarum postulaverat et acceperat. Itaque donec parvitatem nostram electioni factae, atque a se approbatae repugnare conspexerant, ipsi modis omnibus insistebant ne onus pro utilitate Ecclesiae nobis impositum abjiceremus. Ubi vero nos tandem cedere perviderunt, conceptam diu flammam clibanus exsaturatus evomuit. Quapropter cernentes sibi fratrum omnium unanimitatem constanter obluctari, ab eorum et nostra sunt continuo communione sejuncti. Unde vobis apostolica partibus vel audisse, vel vidisse me contigerit, aliis duobus libellis concludere, comite vita, studebo. Et ut omnem dubitationis scrupulum legentibus auferam, per singula quaeque personas a quibus mihi haec sunt relata subnectam: melius esse reputans ex toto silere, quam aliquid falsum mendosumve narrare.

Theophilus. Cum Scriptura dicat: Os quod mentitur occidit animam (Sap. I, 11), quare beatus Paulus, una cum Sila carceris custodiae mancipatus, Romanum se esse asseruit, cum non Romanum, sed Judaeum fuisse luce clarius constet?

Desideruis: Absit hoc a fidelium cordibus, ut veritatis praedicator, doctorque gentium, mendacium in aliquo incurrisse credatur! Beatissimus enim Paulus et Romanus erat, et Romanus non erat; Romanus non erat, quia ex Romana urbe oriundus non fuerat. Romanus vero erat, quia omnis Judaica plebs, ut universus pene orbis, sub Romani tunc temporis imperii ditione degebat. Vel etiam propterea quia Romanus excelsus interpretatur, congruentissime justissimeque se Romanum potuit appellare, quia se excelsum esse nullatenus haesitabat, sicut ipse dicit: Nostra autem conversatio in coelis est (Phil. III).

Theophilus. Fateor, valde mihi sunt grata quae dicis, sed ea, quaeso, quae promiseras narrare jam incipe.

Desiderius. Res valde est nova quam narro, et seniorum nostrorum assertione roborata de reverendissimo viro: Appollinare abbate scilicet nostri monasterii, cui, Deo fautore, licet indignus deservio: cujus sanctitas, benignitas, largitas, omnibus pene in hac provincia commorantibus lucidissime patuit. Qui dum quadam die, necessitate cogente, praedia requireret monasterii, venit ad fluvium Lirim; cumque navis deesset qua fluvium transire posset, plenus fide, signaculo sanctae crucis se muniens, accessit ad oram fluminis, atque, ut erat, indutus vestibus, calceatus pedibus, fluvium est ingressus; et ita sicco vestigio ad alteram ripam pervenit, ut nec calceamenta quidem ipsius madefacta viderentur. Animadverte, precor, quantae sanctitatis, quantaeque religionis ac meriti apud omnipotentem Deum iste vir exstitit, cui adhuc pondere gravato corporis concessum est elementum super liquidum ac si super aridam ambulare; ut videlicet apostolorum principi similis hoc in facto habeatur, cum desuper undas, jubente Domino, sicco vestigio gradiebatur.

Theophilus. Animadverto utique et vehementer admiror, cum in nostris temporibus (in quibus juxta Prophetae vaticinium: Defecit sanctus, diminutae sunt veritates a filiis hominum; non est qui faciat bonum, non est usque ad unum [Psal. XIII]) omnipotens Deus talia dignatus est operari.

Desiderius. Si illud, charissime frater, attendas, quod Dominus discipulis suis promittere est dignatus: Ecce ego vobiscum sum omnibus diebus usque ad consummationem saeculi (Matth. XXVIII), laetari potius quam mirari poteris.

Theophilus . Et laetor quidem, et vehementer exsulto; sed, prorsus precor, inchoata prosequere.

Desiderius. Eo quoque tempore quo gens Agarerenorum, devecta classe, late devastavere Italiam, qualiter omnipotens Deus hoc de manibus illorum liberaverit monasterium, non duxi dignum silentio praeterire. Cum igitur omnia circumcirca igne, ferroque consumpsissent, ecclesias etiam sanctissimorum Petri et Pauli adeuntes depraedati sunt. Dein Appiae carpentes iter, Fundanam aggressi urbem, igne eam cremarunt, cunctique in ea commorantes ab eis vel occisi vel capti sunt. Indeque digressi, in vicinia nostri monasterii trans Lirim fluvium applicantes, quia nox jam imminebat terris, castra posuerunt, ut facto mane omne monasterium funditus diruerent, vel quidquid ibi invenire possent, in praedam abducerent: et ut sunt nimis sitientes sanguinem, omnes quos illic reperissent fratres, gladio jugularent. Cumque hoc tam horrendum, tam immane, tamque formidandum periculum esset in monasterio nuntiatum, omnes fratres nimio pavore perculsi, terrae consternati sunt, divinam majestatem obnixe precantes, ut illorum animas benigne recipere dignaretur, quarum corpora tam subitae, tam formidandae morti, peccatis exigentibus, tradere decrevisset: non enim amplius in hoc mundo se victuros credebant, qui tam proximae mortis gladium sibi imminere cernebant. Igitur cum per totam noctem aspersi capita cinere, vigiliis et orationibus essent intenti, reverentissimus vir Apollinaris abbas, cujus superius mentionem feci, Bassatium abbatem, religiosum scilicet virum, per visionem allocutus est, dicens: Nolite timere, ne moestum geratis animum; non enim in hoc tempore ab Agarenis capiemini, nec aliquid damni divina protegente dextera vobis inferre poterunt; sed quantocius revertentes suos adire tentabunt fines; vos autem deinceps securi ac illaesi manebitis, quia sanctissimus Pater Benedictus vestram ab omnipotente Domino salutem obtinuit; ipse enim venit ad adjuvandum vos, nosque omnes cum eo simul. Igitur venerabilis vir Bassatius abbas expergefactus somno, convocatis in unum fratribus, retulit quae vidisset, quaeque sibi revelata fuissent; et ut instanter omnipotentem Dominum deprecarentur admonuit. At illi certi de divina misericordia alacres effecti, laudantes ac benedicentes Dominum, quod reliquum erat noctis, precibus orationibussque consummant. Tanta vero erat serenitas aeris, ut nulla in eo vel tenuis quidem nubecula videretur, cum subito coelum densatur nubibus, tonitrua concrepant, coruscationes ac fulgura crebra micant, tantusque imber effusus est terris, ut Liris fluvius, late redundans, quasi mare videretur. Igitur illucescente diluculo, surgentes a castris barbari accesserunt ad oram fluminis, diligentius perscrutantes si quam forte navim vadumque reperire possent, ut fluvium transmeare valerent: sed cum omnis transeundi spes eis esset ablata, dira incitati barbarie, manus sibi digitosque corrodentes, quod spe frustrati praedae, vacui remanserant, cellas nostri monasterii trans Lirim positas igne cremantes, verso exercitu quantocius abire coeperunt. Cumque ad eum locum pervenissent, quo praedictus Liris fluvius patenti ostio mari influit, omnes quos habebant equos, debilitatis eruribus, praecisis nervis, quia secum ferre nequibant, reliquerunt. Ipsi vero, ascensis navibus, dantesque carbasa ventis, recto cursu sulcantes aequora, Siciliam devenissent, et se celeriter aridam contingere sperarent: repente parvam cernunt naviculam huc illucque inter suas naves liquidas super undas celeriter discurrentem, in qua clericus veneranda canitie et alter monachus sedere videbantur. Et cum ab eis sollicite interrogarentur unde tam laeti, tam alacres, vel tam onusti repedarent? ab Italia se venire professi sunt, ibique omnia igni ferroque tradidisse: domos etiam Petri ac Pauli, nec non Benedicti se exspoliasse gloriati sunt. Et vos, inquiunt, qui estis, qui tam sollicite, tam diligenter, tamque curiose nos interrogare nitimini? Nos, inquiunt, unus Petrus, alter Benedictus vocamur, quorum domos vos invasisse jactatis; sed cujus virtutis, cujusve potentiae simus, quam citissime experiemini. Et his dictis ab oculis eorum ablati sunt. Mox igitur undique furentibus ventis, tumescentibus fluctibus, tanta subito tempestas exorta est ut naves omnes vel collisae inter se vel impulsae scopulis confractae sint. Ita ut ex omni illa paganorum copia vix pauci superfuerint qui suis haec, a quibus missi fuerant, civibus nuntiare potuissent. Et quidem permisit omnipotens Deus ad tempus suas ab eis ecclesias devastari, sed non est passus eos super tanto facinore diutius gratulari. Hoc in facto illud mihi videtur esse impletum, quod beatus P. Benedictus suis olim discipulis promiserat, dicens: Praesentior vobis, dilecti filii, carnis deposito onere, vestrisque per Dei gratiam cooperator existam assiduus. Illud etiam quod B. Petro Dominus intulit, dicens: Tu es Petrus, et super hanc petram aedificabo Ecclesiam meam et portae inferi non praevalebunt adversus eam (Matth. XVI). Non inquit, non valebunt; sed, non praevalebunt: portae enim inferi pagani sunt, haeretici atque Judaei, qui tunc adversus Dei valere videntur Ecclesiam, cum per eos Dominus suos flagellari fideles permittit; sed non praevalebunt, quia omnipotens ac misericors Deus non eos de Ecclesia sua perpetuos sinit habere triumphos. Unde et Apostolus hortatur, dicens: Tribulationem patimur, sed non coangustamur; aporiamur, sed non destituimur; persecutionem patimur, sed non derelinquimur; humiliamur, sed non confundimur; tribulamur, sed non perimus (II Cor. IV).

Theophilus. Placent vehementer quae dicis.

Desiderius. Joannes sanctae recordationis presbyter, qui in nostro monasterio decanatus officio aliquo tempore functus est, vestri postmodum monasterii quod intra Lucensem urbem constructum est, praepositus fuit, qui quantae obedientiae, quantaeque humilitatis fuerit, plures qui eum noverunt monachi et adhuc supersunt, testes existunt. De mirabilibus vero quae per eum divina majestas operari dignata est, quia plura a memoria lapsa sunt, quae recolo, pauca narrabo. Cum idem vir Dei jejuniis, vigiliis, orationibus, maximeque largitati eleemosynarum esset intentus, tantam lacrymarum gratiam Domino largiente promeruit, ut dubium non esset quod illae lacrymae multa apud Deum impetrare valuissent, quae ex tam simplici humilique corde editae fuissent. Cumque fama sanctitatis ejus totam per eamdem urbem claresceret, daemoniaca quaedam, quae graviter vexabatur, ad monasterium cui ipse praeerat adducta est. Et cum ab eis qui eam duxerant, ut pro eo Dominum precaretur, magnis precibus fuisset obstrictus, convocatis fratribus oratorium intravit, atque multis effusis lacrymis preces pro ea Domino fudit, statimque ab ea daemonium effugavit.

Sed neque hoc sileam, quod veridicis viris de eodem venerabili viro narrantibus agnovi, quod videlicet ita clarum est, ut nullis pene, qui intra moenia ejusdem praefatae urbis Lucensis commorantur, occultum sit vel incognitum. Cujusdam namque illustris viri uxor infirmitate detenta jacebat in lectulo, quae adeo crescente languore ad extrema perducta est, ut per tres dies sine sensu, sine voce recubans, velut mortua haberetur. Cumque omnes qui aderant, funditus de ejus vita desperarent, ad Dei hominem missum est, ut pro ea omnipotenti Domino hostias precesque offerre dignaretur. At ille, ut erat benevolus animo, et ad supplicantium vota paratus, mox sacerdotalibus indutus vestibus ad altare omnipotenti Deo sacrificium oblaturus accessit. Igitur cum intra sacra missarum solemnia nomen illius memoraretur, illa in domo propria, longe a monasterio posita, ex lectulo in quo quasi exanimis jacebat, tanquam si ab aliquo vocaretur, respondit. Cumque ab illis qui aderant interrogaretur quid diceret, vel cui responsum dedisset, illa inquit: Dominus Joannes praepositus nunquid non est hic? ipse enim vocavit me, illique respondi. At illi obstupefacti ex tam inusitato, tam celebri, tamque obstupendo miraculo, tum quia illam quae fere exanimis jacuerat, sanam pene et incolumem videbant; tum quia vocem illius tam longe positi audisse se referebat, statim curaverunt ad monasterium nuntios mittere, ut quid servus Dei ageret agnoscerent, et indicarent: procul dubio credentes, quod non abs re mulier tam celeriter in lectulo surrexisset, responsumque dedisset. Cumque illi qui missi fuerant ad monasterii oratorium intrassent, virum Dei invenerunt juxta altare stantem, ac pro ea longinquitatis auctori Domino sacrificium offerentem; et subtiliter notantes horam, repererunt eodem momento, quo intra sacra missarum solemnia nominata est, eam ex lecto surrexisse, responsumque dedisse.

Felicis etiam memoriae S. Alexander papa vir disertissimus ac eruditissimus exstitit: qui primum Lucensem, postmodum vero Romanam Ecclesiam rexit, ex cujus ore ea, quae nunc refero, de eodem venerabili viro audisse me contigit. Cum quodam tempore idem praefatus pontifex febre correptus graviter aegrotasset, et quotidie languore crescente vehementius fatigaretur, repente ei ad memoriam rediit quod fama vulgante de praedicto servo Dei saepius audierat: quod videlicet, quicunque febre detentus hausisset ex aqua quae de manibus ipsius defluebat, dum post missarum solemnia abhueretur, mox recepta sanitate liberaretur. Latenter igitur misit qui sibi ex illa aqua aliquantulum afferre debuissent. Cumque hi, qui missi fuerant, aquam quam postulaverat attulissent, mox ebibit, atque ita repente sanitati pristinae restitutus est, ut nulla in eo languoris illius indicia remanerent.

Alius quoque vir venerabilis vitae, Guinizzo nomine, mente et habitu monachus fuit, qui ex ulteriori Hispania nostrum ad coenobium veniens, in hac vicina silva non parvo tempore vitam solitariam duxit, ubique in omnipotentis Domini Jesu Christi servitio vitam finivit. De quo venerabili viro Joannes abbas monasterii S. Vincentii, siti juxta ortum Vulturni amnis, qui ei familiarissimus fuit, multa miranda mihi, cum adhuc in nostro monasterio praepositurae curam gereret, referre solitus erat. Cujus discipulus Januarius nomine, magnae obedientiae, magnaeque abstinentiae monachus exstitit. Qui dum quodam tempore a magistro suo, venerabili videlicet Guinizzone, ut ferramenta quibus operari soliti erant reficeret, Aquinum missus fuisset, domum fabri ferrarii adiit, atque ab eo eadem ferramenta reparari, data mercede, poposcit. Faber vero ferrarius coepit eum irridere, dicens: Num ex pane et aqua solitarius iste tam rubicundus tamque pinguis exstat. Rubor iste, ut mihi videtur, magis ex vino quam ex latice hausto procedit. At ille: Hodie, inquit, tibi utrum ex natura an ex assidua vini potatione rubore conspergar, ostendam. Cum vero ferrum in ignem missum vehementer ferveret, et faber ferrarius, id acceptum forcipe, super incudem posuisset, ac scintillae, huc illucque undique volantes, totam pene domum illustravissent, casu ferrum ex incude in terram desiliens cecidit. Igitur venerabilis vir Januarius, ferrum ex incude cecidisse conspiciens, inclinans sese, fervens ferrum nuda manu tenuit, et super incudem ponens, malleatorem, ut quantocius id percuteret, hortatus est. At illi qui aderant viso tanto miraculo, nimio pavore perterriti, pedibus ejus provoluti, veniam ex irrisione quam in eum exercuerant, humiliter deprecati sunt. Sicque factum est ut omnis illa irrisio in venerationem versa sit, quam stulti homines in Dei servum procaciter inferre praesumpserant. Itaque cum venerabilis vir ad magistrum, atque ad cellam propterea remeasset, ab eo vehementer correptus est, quod insultantibus cedens, talia in oculis hominum facere praesumpsisset. Cumque ille unde hoc sciret, vel quis sibi indicasset, percunctaretur: Ille, inquit, qui tibi praestitit ut posses facere, mihi etiam ut possim scire.

Theophilus. Cum Dominus dicat: Luceat lux vestra coram hominibus, ut videant vestra bona opera, et glorificent Patrem vestrum qui in coelis est (Luc. XII), quid est quod sancti viri bona sua occultant, et ne ab aliquibus videantur, omni nisu elaborant?

Desiderius. Sancti viri etsi quandoque opera sua ostendant in publico, intentio tamen illorum manet in occulto; per hoc enim quod intus agunt, laudes exterius non requirunt, quia et de bono opere proximis cupiunt praebere exemplum, et tamen, per intentionem, qua soli Deo placere desiderant, semper optant esse secretum. Tunc, inquam, bona sua occultari appetunt, quando ex eorum propalatione nullum animarum lucrum, nullum fraternae saluti emolumentum cernunt adfuturum. Cum autem exinde ad gloriam omnipotentis Dei aliquid se lucrari posse conspiciunt, tunc bona sua declarari ac propalari patiuntur, quia non suam, sed Conditoris sui laudem requirunt.

Theophilus. Satis aperta ratio patet, nec aliquid inde ultra requirendum puto.

Desiderius. Ea quoque quae de hoc egregio viro, videlicet Guinizzone, Joannes religiosus monachus, qui in hac vicina silva sub anachoretica disciplina solitarius commoratur, solitus est referre, dignum duxi huic nostro associare libello; dicebat enim: Quia cum adhuc in Beneventana civitate in suo monasterio degeret, quadam die quidam Dei servus sibi, aliisque fratribus qui ibi aderant, intulerit, dicens: Pro certo sciatis hodie aliquem magnum virum e monachis apud montem Casinum ex hoc mundo migrasse ad Dominum: quod illi audientes, mirati sunt, quod per octoginta ferme milliaria egredientem e corpore animam illius videre potuerit, et non adhibentes fidem, subtiliter studuerunt indagare. Et repertum est eo die illum venerabilem virum emisisse animam, quo praedictus Dei servus Beneventi positus agnovit.

Sed neque hoc tacebo, quod de Mancuso monacho fratribus referentibus agnovi, quem ipse in monasterio positus vidi, nostroque jam tempore defunctus est. Qui cum ex Apuliae partibus conversionis gratia huc venisset, a Richerio abbate nostro praedecessore susceptus, fratrum congregationi sociatus est. Itaque in monasterio corpore, in saeculo mente degens, semper terrena quaeque meditabatur: omne magisterium regularis disciplinae sibi grave et importabile videbatur. Tunc coepit ab abbate licentiam petere, multasque occasiones adinvenire qua patriam parentesque posset revisere. Cumque ab abbate suo saepius fuisset admonitus, ut viam veritatis, quam semel arripuerat, in melius proficiens de die in diem ad finem usque perducere, deposita omnis torporis ignavia, summopere studeret, ne forte juxta sententiam Domini (Luc. IX, 62), aratrum tenens retroque respiciens regno coelorum aptus esse non posset; et ne uxorem Lot imitans in statuam salis versus (Gen. XIX, 16), horrendum cunctis spectaculum praeberet: ille nihilominus (cujus mens semel a maligno obsessa fuerat) nullo modo quiescebat, sed quotidie abbatem fratresque precibus fatigando, ut eum patriam revisere sinerent, omnimode postulabat. Cumque spem redeundi frustratam sibi esse conspiceret, clam de monasterio egressus, more fugacis servi nocturnas tenebras captans, ut canis ad suum vomitum ad patriam, diabolo instigante, reversus est, atque in parentum domo mansitans, saeculariter ibi, ut jamdudum mente conceperat, vivere coepit. Sed cum ab abbate suo per nuntium saepe fuisset admonitus ut ad monasterii claustra rediret, et ille, salutaria monita parvipendens, obtemperare negligeret, ab eodem abbate communione privatus est. Cum itaque non post multos dies paululum languore correptus in lectulo resideret, immanem leonem ingredientem ostium ac contra se aperto ore venientem cernit. At ille ad ingressum ferocis bestiae territus, coepit magnis vocibus clamare, dicens: Currite, currite, quia leo iste me devorare contendit. Leo vero rugiens irruit in eum, et mordens, coxam illius apprehendens, maximum ex ea carnis frustum abstraxit, sicque eum ementatum ac seminecem relinquens disparuit. Cumque plures ad clamorem vocis illius obstupefacti concurrerent, leonem quidem minime viderunt, sed ementatum ac seminecem monachum in terra prostratum invenerunt. Itaque cum eum a terra elevarent, paululum recepto spiritu, cuncta quae sibi acciderant per ordinem pandit, et ut quantocius se ad monasterium reducerent, propinquos ac vicinos obnixe precatus est. Propinquis igitur ejus voto obtemperantibus, ad cellam hujus nostri monasterii, quae contra Asculanum oppidum sita est, eum portaverunt, ibique post paululum recuperata sanitate, huc ad monasterium est reversus, ac ex perpetrata culpa, poenitentia accepta, plures postea in sanctae conversationis habitu vixit annos.

Theophilus. Monachus iste, ut video, idcirco leoni, id est diabolo, visibiliter ad tempus traditus est, ut postmodum invisibiliter ab ejus potestate liberari in perpetuum mereretur.

Desiderius. Vis etiam ut narrem tibi qualiter omnipotens Deus hoc monasterium de tyrannorum manibus semper eripuit, atque ab inimicorum infestatione, meritis beati P. Benedicti, dextera suae divinitatis protexit?

Theophilus. Narra quodlibet nam alacri animo, devota mente attentisque auribus me cunct haec auscultare profiteor.

Desiderius. Pandulphus Capuanus princeps, vir potentissimus ac ditissimus fuit, qui latrocinando, humanum sanguinem fundendo, civitates, oppida ac aliorum praedia circumcirca manentium crudeliter auferens, suo subdidit dominatui: quique stupra, caedes, rapinas distractionesque bonorum ecclesiarum multa per tempora, absque ulla miseratione, insatiabiliter exercuit. Igitur cum plurimas opes Christi ecclesiis diripiens abstulisset, omnia castra, villas ac praedia hujus monasterii cupiditate ductus sacrilega abstulit, ita ut nec unum rusticum qui rura coleret, vel rura quae a rustico colerentur, monachis reliquisset. Insuper etiam omnem thesaurum hujus monasterii auferens asportavit, ac in arce, quam non longe a Capuana urbe, in monte qui S.

Agathae martyris dicitur, construxerat, in qua multa spolia orphanorum, viduarum et ecclesiarum ac pauperum intulerat, condens reposuit. Cum vero jam omnipotens Deus tantis sceleribus finem vellet imponere, et lacrymae et voces pupillorum, viduarum ac pauperum, nec non orationes precesque servorum Dei, in conspectu Divinitatis ejus essent admissae, sicut scriptum est: Cor regis in manu Dei est (Prov. XXI, 1); Conradi imperatoris menti inspiravit, ut ad vindicandas ejus ecclesias ac de tyrannorum manibus eruendas Italiam revisens Romam veniret (anno 1038). Cum igitur magno exercitu congregato Italiam ingrediens Romam venisset, optimos ex latere suo viros Capuam mittere placuit Pandulpho principi, cui, ut bona S. Benedicti injuste a se ablata, omni postposita mora, restitueret, et nobiles vel cujuslibet generis viros, quos captos ac magno ferri pondere connexos multos in carcere detinebat, dimitteret, omnesque res illorum eis festinanter redderet, per eosdem viros voluit imperare; nam voluntas veniendi ad has partes minime animo ejus insederat, si ea perficere posset quae per praefatos viros eidem Pandulpho praecipiebat. Sed Deus omnipotens, qui cor Pharaonis induravit ob multa quae in populum Dei sine causa irrogaverat mala, ut Mosi servo suo signa et prodigia mirabiliter ostendenti non crederet (Exod. X, 1), induravit etiam et cor istius, ne jussioni imperatoriae obediret. Cumque ii qui missi ab imperatore fuerant Capuam venissent, multis cum eodem Pandulpho verbis frustra habitis, ad imperatorem sine effectu reversi sunt. At vero postquam imperator se contemptum a principe vidit, ira commotus, Roma exercitu moto egrediens, Casinum venit, ac ad B. P. Benedicti limina conscendit. Facta hora fratrum capitulum intravit, congregatisque in unum fratribus, ut pro se Dominum precarentur, rogavit; ibique coram eis Deum beatumque Benedictum non ob aliud se ad has partes venisse, nisi ut ejus monasterium de manu crudelissimi tyranni eriperet, testatus est. Deinde benedictione petita inde ingressus Capuam venit; satellites vero praefati principis, qui monasterii bona ejus imperia ad sui usum detinebant, postquam de Augusti adventu certificati cognoverunt, omnes huc illucque fugientes dispersi sunt. Sicque factum est ut monasterium omnia castra, villas ac praedia sibi ablata uno die reciperet, et ea quae ibi ad alienum usum ministri scelerum congregaverant in monachorum potestatem devenirent. Unde eis mihi contigisse videtur illud quod B. P. Benedictus discipulis suis ex inopia panum tristantibus olim praedixerat: Ut hodie minus, crastina vero abundanter haberent. Praefatus igitur Augustus Capuam ingressus, eidem Pandulpho principatus honorem auferens, alterum in locum ejus constituit. Ipse vero in arcem, quam in monte S. Agathae martyris summo studio munierat, ex eadem urbe fugiens, se contulit. Unde divina dispositione contigit ut omnia quae latrocinando, pejerando, multorumque cruorem innoxium effundendo, multa per tempora acquisierat, in spatio unius septimanae amitteret: nihilque sibi ex tot et tantis acquisitis municipiis, praeter arcem quam praediximus, remaneret, et qui multos aliorum natos, suis ablatis rebus, mendicare coegerat, qui ex eo orti sunt usque hodie huc illucque mendicatum pergant. Quae omnia meritis B. Benedicti sibi evenisse quis dubitet, cujus ipse bona, iniqua ductus cupiditate, distraxit.

Theophilus. De hac re minime dubitandum est, quando coram fratribus praefatus imperator non ob aliud, nisi ob defensionem Sancti Benedicti monasterii se Romam transisse testatus est.

Desiderius. Alio tempore (anno 1049) quidam Capuanus, Pandulphus nomine, collectis ex amicis et vicinis undique equitibus, ac non parvo militum numero congregato, castellum hujus monasterii quae Concha dicitur, diabolo instigante, aggredi ac capere conabatur. Qui e Capuana urbe suis cum sequacibus, inclinato jam ad vesperam die, egressus, ut per totam noctem deambulans, antequam dies illucesceret, cunctis adhuc secure illic dormientibus, praedictum castellum aggredi et capere posset, iter arripuit. Cum vero egressi urbe, aliquantulum processissent, atque in eum locum, ex quo ipsi jam non in die, sed in nocte, ne ab aliquibus viderentur, ambulare disposuerant, pervenissent, eis paululum ibi remorantibus, optata nox supervenit. Qui, ut filii tenebrarum, magis tenebras quam lucem diligentes, ac illud quod Dominus in Evangelio dicit: Qui ambulat in nocte, offendit (Joan. XI), minime attendentes, per agrum unius fundi coeperunt ambulare, et ad invasionem praefati castri quantocius properare. Igitur equis calcaribus cruentatis, recto se itinere ire putantes, per totam noctem praedictum agrum discurrentes, circumierunt. Sed operis Dei mirabili dispositione facto mane, ibi se eos ubi se nox ceperat invenerunt; sicque eis quae cupierant frustrati, confusi ac mirabiliter fatigati, ad domum suam vacui sunt reversi.

Alio quoque tempore, dum piscatores hujus monasterii retia in mare, qui pisces ad refectionem fratrum caperent, misissent, Nortmannus quidam, mente tumidus ac inflatus superbia, furibundus spiritu, supervenit, et ut sunt ad rapinam avidi, ad invadenda aliena bona inexplebiliter anxii, comprehensum unum ex piscatoribus, vestimentum ei, quo erat indutus, abstraxit, sibique mox induit; deinde naviculam ingressus, piscatorem cogere coepit, ut retia ex alto educeret, quatenus pisces, qui in eis inventi essent, secum abstrahens deportaret. Cumque piscator renueret, et se pisces ad monachorum, non ad Nortmannorum refectionem capere velle se diceret, valde caesus ab eodem Nortmanno in mare projectus est. Cum vero idem Nortmannus piscium praedae avidus retia ex alto per semetipsum trahere et pisces legere coepisset, subito inde ex navicula cecidit, atque interclusus ab aequore spiritum exhalavit. Sed, mirabile dictu! ante illum unda mortuum projecit in littore quam piscator, qui ab eo projectus in aquas fuerat, vivus natando pervenire potuisset.

Alio etiam tempore, latrones noctu hujus nostri monasterii cellarium ingressi, carnes, caseum, laridumque exinde subripientes suos sacculos impleverant; sed foras egressi, sacculos, quos impleverant, levare conati minime potuerunt; deinde relicta sarcina tentantes fugere, per totam noctem hac illac per claustra monasterii deambulantes, foras egredi nullatenus valuerunt. Igitur facto mane, cum se intra monasterii claustra conspicerent, timore exterriti ac sui reatus conscii, quid facere nesciebant. Tandem reperto inter se consilio, exeuntes per portam monasterii, si quo modo possent evadere, quasi nihil mali perpetrasse viderentur, caeteris se, qui de monasterio ad quodlibet opus egrediebantur, miscuerunt, et lento pede, ne aliqua de eis suspicio oriretur, carpentes iter, haud longiuscule a monasterio substiterant. Cum interea cellarius fratribus solita stipendia praebiturus, cellarium ingrederetur, refertos ante aditum sacculos invenit, et miratus, ignoransque quid esset, quaeque condita requisivit. Cum autem reposita ablata conspiceret, turbatus damno, foras egressus, quidquid perdiderat, in ipsis sacculis reperiit. Qui, vehementer attonitus et jam quid esset intelligens, mox convocatis ad se duobus vel tribus pueris, per viam vergentis deorsum montis, si forte latrunculos qui id admiserant invenire possent, mittere curavit. Illi autem jussa complentes, cum monasterio egressi paululum processissent, repererunt illos juxta stantes in ipso itinere montis. Cumque jam pene pertransissent eos, ac nullam in eos, quia noti erant, suspicionem haberent, cito gressu iter quod ceperant, peregerunt. Illi vero, divinitus exterriti ac velut amentes effecti, coeperunt post eos clamare et dicere: Scimus, domini, quia ut nos comprehendatis venistis; sed miseremini nostri; nihil enim inde asportavimus, sed ablata omnia in ipso cellarii ingressu dereliquimus. At illi, talia audientes, comprehenderunt eos, ligatisque post tergum manibus ad monasterium perduxerunt, atque ita, ut erant connexi vinculis, fratribus praesentaverunt. Praeterea fuerunt nonnulli qui minus circa praeceptum Domini cauti, caedi eos atque ita sic dimitti judicaverunt; caeteri autem, quorum mens pia in Domino erat, et magis erga mandata divina sollicite studentes jussa complere Dominica, solutos vinculis, cibo potuque refectos, liberos abire permittunt. O mira Domini Jesu Christi benignitas, mira pietas, mira quam docuit patientia; cum in Lege scriptum sit (Lev. XIX; Matth. V): Diliges amicum tuum, et odio habebis inimicum tuum; nec non manum pro manu, dentem pro dente, oculum pro oculo, talionem pro talione reddi mandatum sit; ipse diligere inimicos, benefacere se odientibus, salutare non resalutantes, auferenti tunicam dimittere pallium, ac bona pro malis reddere se sequentibus voluit imperare!

Theophilus. Grata mihi fateor nimium esse quae narras.

Desiderius. Res est mirabilis et vehementer stupenda, quam narro, sed ita a pluribus cognita, ut de ea ab aliquo in nullo debeat dubitari. Quodam itaque tempore Sergius magister militum, qui Neapolitanae praeerat urbi, venatum in ipso sancti Paschali Sabbato, pergens silvam suis cum pueris, ut aprum caperet, est ingressus, tensisque retibus ad insequendos eos sese cum canibus huc illucque unanimiter omnes per silvam diffundunt; sed antequam aper a retis laqueo fugiens involveretur, occupatus a venatoribus, confossus captusque est. Cum autem hora jam tardior esset, et sol, ad occasum vergens, umbram atram jam pene induceret terris, praedictus magister militum, ne noctis tenebris occuparetur, sumpta quam ceperat venatione, omni cum clientela domum quantocius repedare coepit; uni tantummodo puero, Pythagorae nomine, ut retia coligeret et se perniciter sequeretur, imperavit. Igitur cum puer, qui relictus fuerat, collectis retibus recto calle suum dominum sequeretur, subito duo monachi reverendi admodum vultus ei se in itinere contulerunt. Cumque timore exterritus, quinam essent inquireret; illi: Ne timeas, inquiunt; tantummodo sequere nos. Cum itaque aliquantulum simul per eamdem silvam graderentur, venerunt ad quemdam locum coenosum valde atque horribilem aspectu; ubique Pandulphum Capuanum principem, cujus superius mentionem feci, qui non longo ante tempore defunctus fuerat, ferreis nexum vinculis atque in illius coeno laci ad gulam usque demersum, ei miserabiliter ostendunt. Interea duo nigerrimi spiritus, retortas ex agrestibus vitibus facientes, per gulam eum ligaverunt, ac in ipsam lacus profunditatem merserunt, iterumque sursum extraxerunt. Cumque haec saepius facerent, praedictus puer Pythagoras, tremula licet voce, eum alloquitur, ut sibi qua de causa talia pateretur ediceret. Ille vero, flens et ejulans, ad verba interrogantis pueri mox tale responsum protulit, dicens: Quamvis, o puer, ex innumeris meis sceleribus mihi plurima et infinita poena parata sit, tamen ob nullam causam hanc quam cernis patior poenam, nisi propter aureum calicem, quem de monasterio S. Benedicti, sacrilega ductus cupiditate, abstraxi, eique etiam moriens reddere neglexi. Sed obnixe deprecor, ac per Jesum Christum Dominum Salvatorem omnium, cujus ego miser praecepta contemnens, in hanc sum voraginem mortis demersus, te obtestor, ut Capuam ad uxorem meam vel ipse pergas, vel nuntium dirigas, qui ei, et tormenta quae patior, et ut calicem monasterio S. Benedicti reddat, insinuet. At ille: Quid prodest, inquit, si ei nuntiavero? non enim quod te vidissem, vel quod talia patiaris, mihi creditura est. Cui ille respondit: Hoc sibi signum ex mei parte denuntia, quod Pandulphus Gualae filius calicem ipsum pro pignore habeat, et ut datis solidis, quos ei debuimus reddere, illum recipiat, atque S. Benedicti monasterio omni postposita mora restituat; sibi celeriter, rogo, insinuare ne differas. Quibus dictis visio illa ab oculis ejus ablata est. Puer vero statim ut domum regressus est, infirmitate detentus intra paucos dies defunctus est; ea vero quae viderat, quaeve sibi dicta fuerant, omnibus ad se venientibus patefecit. Pandulphus etiam ipse, qui causa pignoris calicem apud se habebat, hoc ipso tempore, nescio qua de causa, Neapolim pergens, haec omnia ex ore ipsius Pythagorae se audisse retulit; per quem quoque idem Pythagoras uxori illius omnia quae de viro ejus viderat, vel quae ipse ei mandaverat, Capuae nuntiavit. Illa autem sibi potius quam marito consulens, pretium, quod vir ejus accommodaverat, redderenolens, nec calicem recipere nec monasterio reddere curavit.

Theophilus. Mirandum valde est ac magna cum cautela pensandum cur omnipotens Deus talia huic puero ostendere volui, cum ille qui sibi ostensus est a poena liberatus non est, vel, cum tot tantisque sceleribus occultatis, pro solo aureo calice cruciari visus est.

Desiderius. Quod vir iste in poenis visus est, et tamen uxore calicem reddere parvipendente, a poenis liberatus non est, justo, occulto tamen, omnipotentis Dei judicio factum est, ejusque pia ac benigna providentia in notitiam hominum deducta est, ut videlicet quicunque haec audierit, pertimescat, et a rapinis ecclesiarum mentem manusque compescat; ne et ante mortem sese poenitere non liceat, et post mortem parentibus propinquisque ea, pro quibus ipse a suppliciis liberetur, operari non libeat; sicque fiat ut pro eis supplicia aeterna possideat, qui Dei timore postposito in vita positus nullatenus perpetrare formidat, et jam veniam non mereatur in vita illa qui bonis sanctisque operibus neglexit promereri in ista. Quod vero caeteris facinoribus tacitis, de solo aureo calice judicari visus est, aperte datur intelligi quam fortiter, quam atrociter, quamque miserabiliter pro aliis pluribus, immensisque sceleribus torquebatur, quando parvi calicis rapina tam dire tamque crudeliter cruciabatur. Nam superius retulimus quod idem Pythagorae puero dixerit, quod multa et immensa delictis aliis fuerant sibi praeparata tormenta. Quod vero is, qui cum in suppliciis vidit, continuo languore correptus, non post multum tempus est mortuus, non multum miremur, si illud quod Danieli, viro desideriorum et sommiorum veridico interpretatori, contigit attendamus; nam post visionem spiritualium mysteriorum, continuo aegrotavit, et per dies plurimos, sicut ipse testatur, elanguit (Dan. VIII). Si autem talis tantusque vir spiritualia visa non tulit, sed continuo languore apprehensus per dies plurimos infirmatus fuit, quid mirum, si puer iste curis saecularibus deditus, carnalibus desideriis pressus, visionem spiritualium rerum ferre non potuit, sed infirmitate detentus ad extrema devenit? Sed in his omnibus divina judicia magis metuenda quam indaganda sunt. Quae magna et inscrutabilia sunt, teste Psalmista, qui ait: Judicia tua abyssus multa (Psal. XXXV): testante quoque Paulo, qui dicit: O altitudo divitiarum sapientiae et scientae Dei! Quam incomprehensibilia sunt judicia ejus, et investigabiles viae ejus? Quis enim cognovit sensum Domini, aut quis consiliarius ejus fuit? aut quis prior dedit illi, et retribuetur ei? Quoniam ex ipso, et per ipsum, et in ipso sunt omnia: ipsi gloria et imperium in saecula saeculorum. Amen (Rom. XI).

LIBER SECUNDUS, In quo agitur de miraculis a S. Benedicto aliisve monachis in monasterio Casinensi ope divina factis. Praemisso utcunque primo, ut promiseramus, libello, nunc secundum, Deo auxiliante, scribere aggrediar: in quo caetera, quae supersunt in hoc monasterio, vel a monachis hujus sacri coenobii ubicunque divina largiente clementia his temporibus facta miracula, quae nostrae occurrunt memoriae, curabo concludere.

Cum adhuc essem laicus, et intra annos adolescentiae aetatem ducerem, quae a multis in Beneventana civitate degens audivi de Joanne tunc ejusdem Beneventanae Ecclesiae archidiacono, postmodum vero hujus S. coenobii abbate, silenter non transibo. Cum idem Joannes de illustri prosapia originem duceret, et, quod majus est, religiose vivens omnipotenti Domino omnimodo placere studeret, ita a clero et populo diligebatur, ut omnes ei unanimiter post mortem archiepiscopi ejusdem urbis summum sacerdotium peroptarent. Alter quidam in eadem Ecclesia, Alix nomine, diaconus erat, qui ad adipiscendum pontificum omni nisu aspirabat, nec, quo ordine id assequi posset, quidquam pensi habebat. Sed dum idem Joannes archidiaconus superesset, ad culmen tanti honoris se posse pertingere desperabat. Cumque haec quotidie in animo volveret, vana illum cogitatio haud quiescere permittebat. Cum quadam die uterque secreto in loco consedissent, et nemo alius cum eis esset, sermo inter eos orsus est de hujusmodi miserae vitae fragilitate, de coelestis ac perpetuae vitae jucunditate, de poena peccatorum, ac de gloria sempiterna justorum. Itaque statuerunt inter se hujus gloriam mundi relinquere, ac sanctae conversationis habitum suscipere; et ut magis fidi esse possent, juramento, quod statuerant, firmaverunt. Dein diem decernunt, quo apud castrum Casinum limina B. Benedicti peterent, ac sub ejus magisterii regula Jesu Christo Domino deservirent. Igitur postquam ad statutum diem ventum est, quo ab eis aggrediendum erat iter, Alix, qui aliud animo, aliud gestabat in ore, Joanni archidiacono dixit: Charissime frater, quoniam de rebus meis aliquid adhuc superest, quod secundum Deum ordinare cupio, tu, obsecro, praecede, et mox ut sanctae conversationis habitum susceperis, mihi nuntium mitte: ego autem, his expletis, quanto citius te subsequi curabo. Archidiaconus vero ad monasterium B. Patris Benedicti veniens, mox ut habitum sacrum suscepit, nuntium ut decreverant socio direxit, qui eum sub sanctae institutionis regula jam colla submisisse, et ut ipse celeriter veniret, ut pollicitus fuerat, nuntiaret. At ille mox ut talia audivit, alacer effectus, quod illum, qui sibi in Ecclesia praeeminebat, recessisse cernebat, omnino se ad eum accedere, atque tam arctam ingredi viam posse negavit. Deinde ad acquirendum culmen pontificatus honoris totis viribus nitebatur. Sed omnipotens ac justus Deus aliter quam ipse sperabat disposuit. Nam cum imperator Otho egressus

Germania Italiam intrasset, postquam Romanas res, ut sibi videbatur, disposuit, Beneventum adiit, cui Alix ita familiaris effectus est, ut idem Augustus eum eligi in pontificem, Ecclesia renuente, praeciperet. Postmodum vero imperator Romam rediens, Romanum pontificem eum consecrare rogavit, et consecratum Beneventum remisit; imperator deinde, febre correptus, post aliquos dies divina dispositione defunctus est. Ille vero Beneventum rediens, ne moenibus quidem civitatis appropinquare ausus fuit, sed cum dedecore illo repulso, alium sibi cives pontificem elegerunt. Fecit quidem haec omnipotens Deus ad vindictam malefactorum, laudem vero bonorum, ut qui cupiditati honoris ductus fraudulenter fratrem suum studuit ab Ecclesia pellere, ipse pulsus patria, exsul in alieno solo vitam finiret.

Praeter haec ea, quae sequuntur, Leone venerabilis vitae, qui ante paucos annos defunctus est, et aliis veteranis monachis narrantibus, audivi. Cum igitur idem Joannes aliquantos in monasterio sanctae institutionis regulae explesset annos, petita ab abbate suo licentia. Hierosolymam perrexit, atque in Sinai monte per sex continuos in Dei servitio degit annos. Postmodum vero in Graecia in monte, qui Hagionoros dicitur, aliquanto tempore mansit. Sed ea, quae illo in loco eum vidisse contigit, haudquaquam mihi videntur reticenda.

Quidam namque eremita in eodem monte manens, a paucis vel frequentabatur, vel noscebatur. Dum quadam die frater qui ei ministrabat, et certis diebus victum deferebat, supra memoratum Joannem venerabilem virum ad eumdem Dei servum duxisset, sicut ipse postmodum discipulis suis cum lacrymis solitus erat referre, benigne, ut decebat, ab eo susceptus est, et cum sermo inter eos de coelestis vitae gaudiis diutius agitaretur, servus Dei iis qui advenerant dixit: Venite, fratres, quia jam hora est, alimenta sumamus corporis, ne revertentes in via deficiatis: nec enim jejuni a nobis recedere debetis, propter quem tanti subiistis iter laboris. Et haec dicens, mensam praeparat, prandium apponit. Cum denique, oratione facta, ad mensam consedissent, mirabile dictu! immanis ursus e vicina silva veniens sese ante ora praudentium favum mellifluo mellis ferens exhibuit. Cumque illi valde perterriti fugam inire tentarent, venerabilis eremita ille eos compescuit, et ne terrerentur admonuit, dicens multos esse jam annos, quo sibi omnipotens Deus per bestiam illum saepissime hoc melliflui nectaris donum sua pietate transmiserit. Peracto itaque prandio surgentes e mensa, animo magis satiati quam corpore, percepta benedictione ad monasterium sunt reversi. Post non multos vero dies beatissimus P. Benedictus eidem Joanni per visionem apparuit, et dans ei pastoralem virgam, quam manu gestabat, ut Casinum ad suum monasterium quantocius reverteretur, admonuit.

Facto itaque mane abbati ipsius monasterii religioso scilicet viro, visionem, quam viderat, per ordinem pandit. At ille, ut erat vir providus atque discretus, voluntatem Dei in hac visione cognoscens, intulit, dicens: Frater Joannes, celeriter ad tuum monasterium reverti festina, ne tanto Patri, qui tibi per visionem apparuit, esse inobediens videaris: decrevit enim, ut mihi videtur, omnipotens Deus te suo gregi praeponere, et, ut suas fideliter pascas oves, sua miseratione elegisse. Ille igitur visioni et admonitioni obtemperans, transmarina relinquens arva, Christo duce, reversus est, atque a religiosissimo viro Joanne, qui tunc fratribus praeerat, praepositus factus, non multo post tempore (quia idem abbas corpore jam debilis erat, atque pondus tanti oneris ferre nequibat) consilio et electione cunctorum fratrum, ab eodem venerabili Patre abbas est ordinatus. Ille vero, abbatia relicta, in vicinam silvam secessit, atque ibi usque ad vitae suae terminum solitarius degens in omnipotentis Deis ervitio vitam finivit.

Intera nec ea quae de Felice audivi, monacho videlicet hujus monasterii, silentio sunt praetermittenda. Quodam tempore, nescio qua de causa, ad Teatinam urbem esse me contigit, et cum ab episcopo et clericis illius Ecclesiae benigne et amicabiliter susceptus essem, atque orationis gratia ad orationem me duxissent, facta oratione, ad dexteram ecclesiae me contuli, ibique aediculam et altare conspexi. Cumque episcopum et clericos interrogassem, in cujus honorem altare illud conditum esset, responsum mihi est, in honorem B. Felicis confessoris Christi altare illud esse dedicatum. Cum autem quis fuerit ille Felix inquirerem, dicebant mihi quod monachus Casinensis congregationis fuerit; atque ab abbate suo illis in partibus missus, ut pastoribus egregie praeesset, ibi vitam finivit; et cum ad corpus ejus omnipotens Deus multa mirabilia operaretur, a majoribus suis de loco in quo prius jacuerat levatus, atque in hac ecclesia, sub hoc, ut cernis, altari conditus fuerit. Igitur quoddam memorabile illo in loco nuper ab eo patratum, omnipotente Domino largiente, narrabatur.

Cum quidam caecus ad cuncta obstantia pedes offendens, misericordem Dominum rogaturus, ante ejus altare venisset, et prostratus toto in terra corpore, gemitu ac suspiriis, ut meritis B. Felicis sui misereretur, orasset: mox depulsis caecitatis tenebris, ita sanus et incolumis surrexit ut, mirantibus cunctis, ipse suis oculis lucem coeperit cernere quam semper ab aliis desideraverat audire.

Theophilus. Velim scire si vir iste venerabilis, qui ita claruit, post mortem in hac vita positus aliquod signum de vitae suae merito dederit?

Desiderius. Non quidem hunc venerabilem virum, dum in hoc saeculo vixit, aliquod indicium suarum virtutum dedisse comperi: verumtamen omnipotens Deus plerumque agere consuevit, ut illi qui devota mente illi servire student, licet in carne positi nullum signum suae sanctitatis ostendant, post mortem tamen cujus meriti fuerint, celari minime patiatur, ut dum exstincta illorum corpora ita miraculis coruscare cernuntur, in ipsius servitio humanae mentes acrius accendantur.

Theophilus. Fateor mihi placere quae dicis; sed, quaeso te, inchoata prosequere; ut dum quae valde cupio, audio, ad amorem supernae patriae fessus animus relevetur.

Desiderius. Gregorius quidam, summae religionis monachus, in hoc coenobio dictus est, qui, sicut a plerisque hujus loci fratribus audisse me reminiscor, dum in praesenti vita moratus est, sub monasticae disciplinae regula omnipotenti Domino studuit strenuissime deservire. Cumque expleto vitae termino ex hoc mundo migrasset, tanta odoris fragrantia de loco in quo exanimis jacebat emanavit, ut omne subito monasterium illius odoris suavitas, quasi unius angulum domatis mirifice resperserit. Et dum omnes odoris illius ineffabili quadam suavitate recreati mirarentur, ac quid esset omnino nescirent, nuntius repente ab infirmorum domo properans venit, qui Gregorium monachum obiisse retulit. Voluit itaque omnipotens Deus ostendere quanti meriti iste vir fuerit, cujus egrediente anima tam mirifico odore coenobium omne repleverit.

Alter quidam, ut fratres qui adhuc supersunt referunt, Angelus, in hoc monasterio monachus, dictus est, cujus profecto vita nomini dissimilis non fuit. Qui dum infirmitate tactus corporis ultimum diem clausisset, daemoniacus quidem forte in coquinam intraverat: et ecce subito coepit strepere, ac se, furibundus a terra dissiliens, in aera elevare, magnisque vocibus clamans, cum se a Benedicto perpeti conquerebatur, dicens: O quid nunc mihi modo Benedictus fecit; animam Angeli monachi, ob parvum cucullum quod gestavit in capite, mihi auferens secum detulit. Cumque omnes qui aderant ad verba illius stupefacti intenderent, et quid diceret ignorarent, repente signum, quo fratrum obitus significari solet, insonuit: statimque fratres omnes festinanter ad domum infirmorum pergunt, et Angelum monachum jam defunctum reperiunt. Qua de re aperte monstratum est, quod animae illius in aliquo nocere non potuit, de cujus morte coram fratribus tam tristem, tam lugubrem se antiquus hostis ostendit.

Theophilus. Quaeso ut dicas cur diabolus tantum inimicetur humano generi, ut ab ortu nativitatis usque ad exitum vitae omnibus modis elaboret a mandatis Creatoris sui hominem avertere, atque ad aeternam patriam tendenti quascunque poterit insidias tendere.

Desiderius. Aperta ratio patet, quod antiquus hostis, qui se Creatori suo aequiparare contendit, passus magnam ruinam, in voraginem profundi barathri demersus sit; et idcirco humano generi omnibus modis contrarius existat, quia illuc eum ascendere cernit, unde ipse per superbiam dejectus irrecuperabiliter cecidit: inde est quod strepere, insanire, frendere in electorum Dei transitu terribiliter videtur.

Azzo etiam quidam religiosae satis vitae monachus fuit, qui ecclesiam B. Michaelis archangeli in valle quae dicitur Regis, a Ludovico Christianissimo imperatore mirifico opere constructam, postmodum vero a Saracenis destructam omni cum studio restauravit, ibique fratres ad omnipotentis Dei servitium, prout potuit, congregavit. Cumque ibidem in servitio Dei complesset annos, ultimam jam pene agens aetatem, ad monasterium nostrum, ex quo ab abbate suo missus fuerat, est reversus. Qui senio morboque confectus in domo infirmorum, in lectulo jacens, extremum vitae spiritum jam moriturus trahebat, multique e fratribus excubantes circa lectum ipsius hymnis et psalmis vacantes, ejus exitum exspectabant. Quidam vero frater, qui adhuc superest, et nobiscum in monasterio conversatur, tunc juvenis, nunc autem aetate moribusque grandaevus, in dormitorio cum caeteris fratribus quiescebat: cum ecce subito nocte intempesta respiciens, vidit per visionem B. Michaelem archangelum, cujus vultum pictura eum docente cognoverat, per dormitorium venientem: cujus alter angelus vestigia subsequens paulo longius gradiebatur; quem intuens dixit: Domine, nonne tu B. Michael archangelus? Et ille: Ego sum utique. At ille: Quo tendis, inquit, domine? Ad domum, inquit, infirmorum, ut fratrem Azzonem mecum assumam, quia jam tempus est, pergo. Et his dictis, visio quam videbat disparuit. Qui statim evigilans surrexit, et festinanter ad domum infirmorum perrexit, fratremque Azzonem e corpore animam jam exhalasse invenit. Qua de re aperte datur intelligi quod idem B. Michael eum secum detulerit, qui ad assumendum eum se venisse testatus est.

Frater quidam in nostro monasterio Stephanus Veneticus dicebatur, qui ex Venetiae partibus adveniens, in sanctae conversationis habitu studiosissime vixit, cujus humilitatis, patientiae ac obedientiae bonum omnibus, qui tunc in omnipotentis Dei servitio ibidem congregati erant, liquidissime patuit. Cumque jam tempus esset ut ejus digna conversatio a justissimo Domino remunerari debuisset, molestia gravatus corporis, fratribus coram positis, diem clausit extremum. Tunc quaedam religiosissima anus, Agundia nomine, virgo mente et corpore, quae in sanctimoniali habitu juxta ecclesiam Beatae Mariae semper Virginis sitam in civitate quae circa radicem Casini montis est condita, manebat more solito, antequam clerici ejusdem civitatis ad reddendas nocturnas Deo laudes surrexissent, ante praedictam ecclesiam Dei genitricis stans, gemitu, lacrymis ac suspiriis omnipotentem Dominum precabatur, cum ecce subito intempesta noctis hora respiciens, vidit columnam igneam e cella, in qua infirmi fratres quiescere erant soliti, exeuntem, coelumque tendentem. Quae mox nuntium monasterium subire praecepit, qui studiose inquireret si aliquis ex infirmis fratribus in cella illa degentibus ex hoc mundo migrasset. Tum is, qui fuerat missus nuntius, perniciter montem ascendit, monasterium intravit, domum infirmorum adiit, atque Stephanum religiosum monachum defunctum reperiit: et studiosius inquirens, invenit eum ea hora emisisse animam, qua columna ignea ab ancilla Dei visa est celsa penetrare polorum.

Alter quidam in jam dicto nostro monasterio Joannes Veneticus dictus est, mirae patientiae, obedientiae ac humilitatis monachus, qui quanti meriti apud Jesum Christum Dominum fuerit, suum post obitum manifestissime claruit. Cum quidam frater, cujus nomen a memoria excidit, casu in inguine crepuisset, ita ut interiora ejus, membrano disrupto, inter carnem et corium dilaberentur, sepulcrum ipsius adiit, ac se super illud prosternens, lacrymis gemitibusque, ut pro se Dominum precaretur, ex intimo cordis postulabat affectu: procul dubio credens ejus meritis se posse sanitatem recipere, qui in hac vita positus omnipotenti Domino totis viribus studuit deservire. Cum igitur aliquantulum super sepulcrum ejus orans incubuisset, ita restitutus est sanitati, ut languoris pristini nec ullum in eo quidem indicium remansisse videretur.

Smaragdus monachus, qui adhuc superest, et in nostro monasterio commoratur, retulit mihi quod narro. Quod a Leone venerabili presbytero, avunculo scilicet suo, se audisse referebat de Antonio monacho atque presbytero. Qui saecularibus ac divinis litteris haud mediocriter eruditus, ab adolescentia usque ad vitae exitum in saepedicto monasterio degens, omnibus pene in hac provincia notus exstitit. Qui dum quodam tempore, casu accidente, sicut praedictus presbyter ex ore illius accepit, loco in secretiori crepuisset, et languore crescente quotidie vehementer fatigaretur, medicum, a quo secari vel exuri deberet, si quo modo posset sanitatem recipere, conducere meditabatur. Timebat tamen si secaretur a medico, ut multoties evenire solet, ne forte moreretur, et rursus si non secaretur, sedulum sustineret dolorem, quod est ipsa morte deterius, periculosius sibi videbatur. Igitur cum intra se haec diutius agitaret, unum sibi fore remedium credidit, ut ad sepulcrum beati Benedicti pergens ipsius misericordiam imploraret, sperans se ejus patrocinio posse salvari, sub cujus magisterio se recedens a saeculo devotissime contulerat. Statim igitur ecclesiam intravit, ac se coram altari humiliter prosternens, diutius oravit, ut omnipotens Deus meritis tanti Patris salutem sibi conferre dignaretur. Expleta vero oratione, e pavimento, in quo prostratus jacuerat, surrexit, atque ex crepidine altaris pulverem collegit, et ligans in panno, loco in quo patiebatur superimposuit: atque die altero ita sanus repertus est, ut nec signum quidem praeteritae infirmitatis in eo omnimodo remaneret.

De Paulo sanctae conversationis monacho quod a fratribus, qui adhuc in hac praesenti vita vivunt, et eum optime norunt, audisse me memini, referre curabo. Cum idem Paulus salutis suae causa nostrum ad coenobium devenisset (anno 1022), a Theobaldo abbate, religioso videlicet viro, qui tunc fratribus honestissime praeerat, devote susceptus est. Quem venerabilis Pater in monasterio beati Patris Benedicti, quod intra Capuanam urbem constructum est, habitare praecepit: qui postquam ad eumdem pervenit, ita se sub sanctae institutionis regula constrinxit, ut ob hoc omnibus mirabilis haberetur. Sed omnipotens, misericors ac pius Deus, quantum sibi ejus digna conversatio in hac vita placuerit, illius post obitum ostendere est dignatus. Cum namque in eodem monasterio religiosam, honestam ac dignam Deo conversationem exercens, aliquantos explesset annos, infirmitate pulsatus corporis et carnis ergastulo, jubente Domino, exilivit. Igitur quidam venerabilis vitae episcopus ex Galliae partibus veniens, orationis gratia ad ecclesiam Beati Michaelis archangeli in Cargano monte conditam properabat. Cum autem ad Capuanam urbem devenisset, juxta ecclesiam protomartyris Stephani diversus, hospitatus est. Denique cum nocte intempesta e lectulo surrexisset, ante ecclesiam praedicti martyris stans, vicinas sibi omnipotentis Dei aures precibus, lacrymisque reddebat: cum ecce subito, ad dexteram orientis partem oculos porrexisset, vidit instar solis radiis lucem splendidam e monasterio per aera mirabiliter advolare. Cumque diu lucem quam videbat attonitus miraretur, signum in monasterio insonuit, quo fratris exitus significabatur. Intellexit protinus e fratrum numero aliquem magni meriti ex hoc mundo migrasse, simulque cum ipsa luce coeli sublimia penetrasse. Mox itaque convocatis clericis, quae viderat enarravit, statimque ad monasterium nuntium misit, ut quis ibi defunctus esset agnosceret. Cumque is, qui missus fuerat, monasterium intrasset, invenit Paulum venerabilem monachum e corpore animam emisisse.

Joannes admodum religiosus monachus, et sacerdos, cujus superius mentionem feci, qui, relicto regimine monasterii, ad Eremi secreta se contulit, in hac vicina silva usque ad extremum vitae suae terminum solitarius mansit: ibique jejuniis, vigiliis ac orationibus operam dans, studuit omnipotenti Domino sollicita mente servire. Hic vero cum temporibus Theobaldi abbatis ex hac luce migrasset (anno 1022), monachus quidam Joannes nomine, in monasterio Beati Laurentii martyris, quod apud Capuam est, studiosissime in Dei servitio conversabatur: qui dum quadam nocte antequam fratres ad vigilias surgerent, de lectulo, more solito, omnipotentem Dominum precaturus surrexisset, dum attenta mente stans misericordem Dominum precaretur, subito respiciens clarissimam lucem in aere et intra ipsam venerabilis viri Joannis animam coelum penetrare conspexit. Igitur facto mane, certius scire volens quod viderat, venit ad Andream, qui cellae hujus monasterii, quae intra eamdem Capuanam urbem sita est, tunc praepositus erat, hocque, quod viderat, per ordinem retulit: et ut ad hoc monasterium nuntium dirigeret, qui diligentissime rem quam viderat investigaret, obnixe poposcit. Qui ejus voto parere studens, nuntium mox direxit, qui diligenter haec quae dicta sunt cognosceret, citiusque reversus indicare curaret. Tum is qui missus fuerat nuntius, dum festinanter pergeret, et in ipso itinere alter a monasterio veniens occurrit, qui fratribus in praedicta cella Capuae commorantibus praefati servi Dei obitum nuntiavit; a quo subtiliter inquirens, invenit praedictum Dei servum ea hora ex hac luce subtractum, qua eum Joannes religiosus monachus, Capuae positus, coelum mirabiliter penetrasse cognovit. Tunc uterque ad eos a quibus missi fuerant reversi, alter servi Dei obitum, alter vero visionem, quae de eo visa est, retulerunt.

Multorum fratrum testimonio didici haec, quae nostro curavi annotari libello. Et licet Petrus venerabilis Ostiensis episcopus in sermone, quem in vigiliis B. Patris Benedicti legendum luculentissime composuit, id eleganter decenterque inseruerit, tamen inter caetera miracula, quae omnipotens Deus ad laudem sui nominis nostra etiam memoria, vel seniorum nostrorum, quos ipsi vidimus, quibusque referentibus, agnovimus, hoc in nostro monasterio ostendere est dignatus, inserere curavi, ut in cujus forte manus sermo ille non venerit, et hoc in nostro libello cognoverit, Deum laudet in mirabilibus suis, qui omni tempore, novo videlicet cibo alit teneras mentes suorum. Igitur quodam tempore ab initio Maii mensis usque ad extrema mensis Julii, tanta siccitas aeris exstitit, ut ne paucissimis quidem guttis arens terra, et crebris discissa rimis, aliquo modo madefieri videretur. Tunc quadam die quidam rusticus, ut stipulam triticeae messis suo in agello succenderet quo liberius terram excolere posset, allatum ignem incaute supposuit; cumque ignis paulatim stipulam lambendo flammam in alto porrigeret, flante aura in proximam silvam, quae subjacet monasterio, rustico renitente, dissiluit. Igitur infinitam sibi silva ministrante materiam, ignis huc illuc per latera montis discurrens, omne monasterium incendio se concrematurum, populis undique spectantibus, minabatur. Cum itaque fratres flammis crepitantibus timore exterriti atque turbati, animo expergefacti, a lectulis surrexissent (nam in meridiano tempore illis quiescentibus res ista contigerat), videns tam immane, tam subitaneum periculum, et ei qualiter resistere possent nullo modo excogitare valentes, ad divina se statim contulere praesidia. Totis itaque viribus et ex intimo cordis affectu omnipotentem Dominum rogare coeperunt, ut meritis B. Patris Benedicti, quo ordine vellet, sua virtute monasterium ab incendio eriperet, quod humana manu defendi posse penitus desperabant. Cumque alii erectis in coelum manibus, atque alii prostratis in terra corporibus, alii flexis genibus, alii in terram demissis capitibus omnipotentem Dominum precarentur, subito parva nubecula se in hujus latere montis colligens, supra cacumen ipsius, divina imperante potentia, dilatavit; quae mox tantum imbrem ex se effundens expressit, ut et incendium omne exstingueret, et omnino monasterium liberaret. Studeamus igitur, fratres, religiose ac pie vivere, et tantum patronum, Deo serviendo, propitium acquirere: quia cujus meritis nubes hujus cacumen montis obtexit, atque ex se copiosum imbrem exprimens, incendium exstinxit, ejus nihilominus precibus, si eum sedule ac devote, praeveniente bono opere, rogaverimus, ab aestuantium vitiorum flamma, divina concedente misericordia, liberabimur.

Quodam tempore, sicut ab iis qui optime noverant agnovi, dum fratres hujus monasterii ecclesiam B. Scholasticae virginis intra Cajetanam urbem, quatenus dum ad aliquas res emendas ibidem pergerent, receptaculum habere possent, construerent; quidam ex operariis in summitate rupis, quae in capite civitatis mari praeeminet, saxa quibus ecclesiae parietes construerentur, frangebat. Qui cum attentius eadem saxa malleo quateret, idem malleus de manubrio recidit, ac per ingens praecipitium, quod ibidem patebat, delapsus in mare cecidit; qui valde contristatus quod evenerat damno, ad fratres ubi parietes ecclesiae aedificabant, protinus venit, et ea, quae sibi acciderant, moerens retulit. Cumque spes recuperationis esset ablata, et alterum sibi malleum, quo saxa ad ecclesiae aedificium frangerentur, fieri decreverant, unus e fratribus dixit: Descendamus illuc, fratres, forsitan B. Benedictus suis meritis nobis malleum restituet, qui quondam Gotho ferramentum ex profundo lacus mirabiliter abstrahens reddidit, atque ad opus quod coeperat, laetum remisit. Placuit sermo coram caeteris, et descendentes ad mare naviculam sunt ingressi: regyrantesque sinum civitatis, venerunt ad locum in quo sub praedicto praecipitio ex operarii manibus dissiliens malleus ille ceciderat: in quo videlicet tanta erat aquarum profunditas, ut spes recuperandi illum per aliquod humanum ingenium nulla omnino persisteret. Igitur confisi de omnipotentis Dei adjutorio et meritis B. Patris Benedicti, manubrium in aequora mittunt. Mirum in modum, mox ferrum manubrio adhaesit, et extrahentes eum foras, gratias agentes Deo et B. Benedicto gaudentes ad opera sua sunt reversi.

Theophilus. Hoc miraculum et in Veteri Testamento ab Eliseo, et in Novo a sanctissimo P. Benedicto factum reminiscor. Sed dum merita istorum illorumque longe distantia esse perpendo, majorem, fateor, admirationem de hoc nuper patrato miraculo in animo meo concipio.

Desiderius. Hoc factum, charissime frater, non tantum istis imputare debemus, quantum illi, de cujus meritis confisi, id agere tentaverunt. Verumtamen vis narrem aliquid de obsessis a daemone, divina largiente clementia, suffragantibus B. Benedicti meritis in hoc ejus monasterio curatis, ut audientium animus magis ac magis in Dei laudibus convalescat, atque in amorem summae divinitatis multipliciter incalescat.

Theophilus. Quidquid ad aedificationem audientium dicere velis, prosequere: ego autem me haec gratanter auscultare profiteor.

Desiderius. Quidam puer in domo hospitum simul cum patre in lectulo cubans, cum ad necessitatem corporis in ipso noctis silentio surrexisset, subito ingens leo dentibus fremens, eum paratus discerpere unguibus, sibi horrendus apparuit; qui pavore nimio exterritus vociferans, in terram corruit. Ad cujus vocem mox turbatus pater e lecto surrexit, festinus ad eum, valdeque anxius accessit, cur ita clamasset, vel quid sibi evenisset, prima diligentia sollicitus interrogavit. Ille immanem leonem contra se venientem tremebundus ac palpitans vidisse se retulit. Quem pater blanditiis demulcens, in ulnis propriis acceptum reduxit ad lectulum. Sed diabolus, qui in specie leonis sibi apparuerat, in eum ingressus, post aliquot dies vehementissime vexare coepit. Cumque ad ecclesiam ante altare Beatissimi Benedicti esset adductus, mirum in modum, in pavimento clausis oculis prostratus jacens, quicunque monasterii portam ingrediebatur, mox ejus nomen exprimebat, dicens: Talis, vel talis homo per portam modo monasterii ingreditur. Quidam autem frater cum causa obedientiae e monasterio ad civitatem descendisset, duodecim a quodam accipiens denarios, eosque propriae utilitatis gratia occulte capiens sibi in sinum misit. Cum autem ad monasterium reversus, ad puerum in locum, quo vexabatur, accessisset, statim diabolus hoc modo eum per os pueri coram fratribus infamare coepit, dicens: Monachus iste contra regulam sui ordinis duodecim denarios a tali viro accipiens causa proprii commodi, occultatos retinet in sinu. Igitur cum a fratribus interrogaretur utrumnam vera essent convicia quae antiquus hostis per os vexati sibi objiceret, mox ille suam clamitans culpam, omnino id ita esse professus est.

Alter quoque frater, cujus nomen, ne verecundiam patiatur, omitto, ex alio monasterio suae salutis causa ad nostrum deductus, quadam nocte ad nocturnas vigilias, lectionem de Veteri Testamento in ecclesia, more solito, fratribus residentibus, recitabat, cum forte puer qui vexabatur, aderat. Et ecce subito diabolus per os ejus exclamans, illa omnia quae legebantur sese ad liquidum nosse, ibique fuisse protestabatur; et adjungens hujusmodi lectoris verbis exprobrabat: Sed si ea, inquit, quae de te scio, referre coram praesentibus vellem, magnam profecto tibi verecundiam incutere possem. Et revera fratrem illum abunde in suo monasterio saeculariter vixisse compertum est. Postquam igitur pro vexato puero ante sepulcrum B. P. Benedicti diutius a fratribus oratum fuisset, ita sanus effectus est, ut amplius a maligno spiritu vexari minime visus esset.

Eodem etiam tempore alter puerulus ingentem Aethiopem super tectum stantem conspexit, qui valde territus, mox fugam arripit. Sed idem daemon eum insequens ad ostium domus, in terram prostravit, statimque in eum ingrediens, acriter miserum fatigabat. Cumque in oratorium ad sepulcrum praedicti Patris per aliquot dies saepe fuisset adductus, ejusdem Patris meritis, qui eum invaserat daemon relinquens abscessit, sic ut ad eum accedere ulterius ausus non fuerit.

Alius quidam, Joannes nomine, qui aetate provectus adhuc superest, atque in infirmorum domo deservit ex provincia Marsorum, de qua ortus fuerat, cum a pessimo daemone teneretur, hoc ad coenobium gratia recuperandae salutis a propinquis adductus est, procul dubio credentibus eum meritis B. Benedicti salutem posse recipere, ad cujus limina multos diversis languoribus occupatos audierant saluti pristinae restitutos. Et ipse post non longum tempus expulso hoste, sanitate recepta, magnam exsultationem videntibus intulit.

Theodoricus etiam monachus atque sacerdos, qui adhuc vivit et nobiscum in hoc coenobio religiosam vitam ducens, conversatur, nepotem habuit, quem valde diligebat in saeculo; in quem antiquus hostis ingressus est, non tamen ut aperte eum vexaret, sed latenter languorem inferens, quasi paralyticum videntibus exhiberet. Hunc itaque praedictus avunculus ejus causa recuperandae sanitatis ad se, de B. P. Benedicti confidens meritis, adduci fecit. Sed cum in hoc monasterio aliquandiu infirmus ita ut vexerat, perduraret, et a nullo, quod eum daemon possideret, aestimaretur, quadam die ab eodem avunculo suo ad venerabilem virum, Lambertum nomine, qui in hac proxima silva juxta ecclesiam SS. Martyrum Cosmae et Damiani solitarius habitabat, ut ejus benedictione frueretur, delatus est. Cui vir Dei panem benedictum dedit, eumque ut comederet, imperavit. Cumque sibi, quod acceperat in os misisset, idque comedens gustasset, daemon, qui hactenus in eo latuerat, benedictionem tanti muneris ferre non valens, strependo, vociferando, huc illucque dissiliendo, quae causa languoris esset, innotuit. Postquam vero cum avunculo ad monasterium est reversus, et aperte quod a daemone possideretur cognitum fuit, ductus in oratorium est, quo omnipotentem Dominum pro eo rogaturi cuncti simul fratres conveniunt. Expleta itaque oratione ac psalmodia, hora sexta fratres ad refectorium, dimissis cum eo duobus vel tribus monachis, causa reficiendorum corporum, pergunt. Igitur cum illi, qui remanserant, divinam pro eo misericordiam lacrymabiliter precarentur, quatenus intercessione beatissimi confessoris sui Benedicti liberare captivum hominem dignaretur, monachus veneranda canitie eidem, qui vexabatur, ante altare stare visus est: qui antiquo hosti ab eo recedere potenti virtute imperabat. Mox daemon, facto impetu magno, cum vomitu ab obsesso exiit, atque ad eum ulterius accedere minime praesumpsit. Quem videlicet senem B. Maurum procul dubio fuisse compertum est, cujus reliquias, fratres qui cum eodem obsesso in ecclesia remanserant, super pectus ejus magna cum devotione ac spe posuerant. Is autem, liberatus a daemone, est monachus factus, et in hoc monasterio caeteris cum fratribus in Jesu Christi Domini nostri servitio perseverans existit.

Rusticus quidam in vicinia hujus monasterii in castello, quod Sancti Angeli nominatur, habitabat: qui festivitatem B. Nicolai confessoris Christi per annos singulos una cum familia sua, prout poterat, devotissime celebrabat. Ea igitur die, qua ejus sacra a fidelibus colebatur solemnitas, ad basilicam illius nomini consecratam, cum uxore et filio, in puerili adhuc aetate manente, oblationem Domino oblaturus, accessit. Postquam vero expletis missarum solemniis, et communione sacri corporis et sanguinis Domini participati, ad domum propriam sunt reversi, puer a patre agrum revisendi licentiam petiit. Quem pater compescuit, dicens: Non est dignum, o fili, in agrum hodie ad agri opus exercendum exire, quia, licet indigni, divina sacra percepimus, et festivitas patroni nostri, beatissimi scilicet Nicolai, ab omnibus magna cum devotione ubique recolitur. Sed ille puerili levitati deditus, postquam quod petierat a patre impetrare nequit, paterna jussa parvipendens, clam de domo avolans, solus ad rura visenda contendit. Ubi vero aliquandiu in agro moratus, solem ad occasum vergere, et opacam noctem jam pene terris imminere conspexit, ad vicinam silvam, ne vacuus redire videretur, ac per hoc patris gratiam, cujus verba contempserat, recipere posset, ligna caesurus, domumque delatuturus accessit. Cumque ligna jam componere coepisset in sarcinam, subito quasi vehemens spiritus sonitum contra se venire persensit; elevatoque sursum capite, nigerrimam avem in modum vulturis, magno cum impetu per aera super se volantem conspexit, quae haud longiuscule in semita qua puer regredi debebat sese obviam posuit. Itaque cum timore perterritus ac tremebundus in eam intenderet, illa in speciem nigerrimi pueri, cujus capilli hispidi ac sursum erecti, extrema pars vestium in ruborem desinere videbatur, sese transformans, ostendit. Igitur puer, dum id quod videbat, pavidus ut erat, animo inspiceret, idem antiquus hostis eum taliter allocutus est: Efficere, inquit, o puer ex toto meus, et una mecum ad hujus proximi fluminis oram accede; ibique auri et argenti magnam copiam tibi tribuam, ut non lignis, sed auro, argentoque domum revertaris onustus, quatenus, dum superfueris, omnes propinquos vicinosque tuos divitiis excellens, nobiliter deliciosiori vita fruaris in terris. Haec autem ei antiquus hostis non ideo persuadebat, ut quae pollicebatur tribueret, sed ut eum mergens necare posset in flumine. At puer, frequens Christi nomen invocans, crucis se studebat munire signaculo; flebilique voce talia responsa reddebat: Absit a me, absit, ut alicujus aliquando efficiar famulus, nisi, qui me creavit, omnipotentis Dei, et qui me generavit, patris mei. Cum itaque iterum atque iterum signum salutis sibi apponeret, daemon, qui videbatur, in undas vicinas fluminis inde se submovens, magno cum strepitu se mersit, ibique serpentum sibilare, asinorum rudere, mugire taurorum, rugire leonum more coepit, atque tantum timorem misello incussit, ut tota sibi silva rotari in vertiginem videretur. Cumque in terra fere jaceret exanimis, et quid ageret penitus ignoraret, ecce subito senex mitrato capite, candidus, indutus stola, sibi astans apparuit, et inquit ad eum: Quid hic agis, cum se jam hora tardior protrahat, et recedentibus cunctis solitaria jam pene arva remanserint? Surge quantocius, domumque redire festina, ne si amplius hic moratus fueris, grave periculum incurras. Surgens itaque de terra, cum ad se levandam sarcinulam inclinasset, idem qui visus fuerat senex disparuit. Et ecce iterum malignus spiritus ante oculos ejus se ingerens, eisdem quibus prius, verbis affari puerum coepit. Sed ille nihilominus quae hortabatur, se facturum omnino denegans, flens et ejulans in terram decidit, ac prout poterat et sciebat, Salvatoris omnium Jesu Christi clementiam, ut sibi praeberet auxilium, flagitabat. Mox ille venerandus senex, qui ei dudum visus fuerat, rursus apparuit, et ut citius surgeret, lignaque auferens, asportaret, hortatus est. Ad cujus adventum, inimicus qui videbatur, ut fumus evanuit. Quem utique senem, beatum fuisse credimus Nicolaum, cujus celebrandae festivitati praedictus rusticus eo die operam dederat. At puer ad senis imperium surgens e terra, levata sarcinula, summa cum velocitate domum rediit, et ut ipse postmodum referebat, tam levi sibi illa lignorum sarcinula facta est, ut nihil ponderis habere videretur. Cum autem domum regressus paululum remoratus esset, qui ei apparuerat daemon in eum ingressus coepit horribiliter fatigare. Uterque turbatus parens affuit, lugens et perstrepens familiola cuncta circumstetit. Sed eum nullum ei auxilium impendere posse se cernerent, salubri reperto consilio, hoc ad monasterium ad limina eum B. Benedicti perducunt, atque ad ejus venerandum sepulcrum in dextera parte altaris, misericordiam Domini lacrymabiliter postulantes, prosternunt, ibique obsessus vehementer fatigatus obdormivit. Igitur dum sic fessus dormiens jaceret, aperiri sibi subito a latere visum est, indeque vir clarissimo aspectu candidoque amictus habitu procedens, ejus alvum, pectusque diu contrectans, ei, ut surgeret ac discederet, imperavit. Qui mox expergefaetus, ita sanus surrexit ut daemoniacam infestationem in se ulterius non sentiret. Haec omnia per ordinem, ex ore ipsius pueri, qui passus fuerat, lacrymabiliter referentis, audivi.

Theophilus. Haec quae puero contigisse narras, valde admiror, atque ad omnipotentis Dei judicia tremens stupesco, cur illum, qui una cum patre festivitatem B. Nicolai devote celebrans, communionem Dominici corporis et sanguinis percepit, immundo spiritui mancipare permiserit.

Desiderius. Si animadvertas utique quantum parentibus non obedire delictum sit, cum Scriptura dicat: Honora patrem tuum et matrem tuam, ut sis longaevus super terram (Exod. XX, 12). Et item: Melius est obedire quam sacrificare, et auscultare magis quam offerre adipem arietum, quoniam quasi peccatum ariolandi est, repugnare; et quasi scelus idololatriae, nolle acquiescere (I Reg. XV, 23, 24). Et Salomon: Audi, fili mi, disciplinam patris tui, et non dimittas legem matris tuae, ut addatur gratia capiti tuo, et torques collo tuo (Prov. I, 8, 9). Et alio loco: Quam malae famae est, qui relinquit patrem, et est maledictus a Deo qui exasperat matrem (Eccli. III, 18). Justo Dei judicio id accidisse probabis. Permisit itaque Deus puerum hunc pro sua inobedientia flagellari: sed solita pietate non est passus eum sub eodem verbere diutius immorari, ut ex hoc quisque intelligat quantum inobedientia periculum pariat, atque ad obediendum parentibus quantum sese humiliter subdere debeat.

Theophilus. Verba responsionis tuae satisfecisse videntur interrogationi meae.

Desiderius. In dioecesi Teatini episcopatus est monasterium nobile juxta radicem Majellici montis, in honorem sancti Liberatoris constructum, et huic nostro Casinensi coenobio subditum, ubi magna fratrum multitudo commorantes, juxta almi B. Benedicti mandatum, Christo Domino vero Regi militantes deserviunt.

Quodam igitur tempore, dum fratres in eodem monasterio in noctis silentio juxta morem quiescerent, quidam reverendus vir monastico indutus habitu apparuit uni eorum, eumque exhortans ut velociter de lectulo in quo jacebat surgeret. Cumque ille ad ejus imperium expergefactus perniciter surrexisset, inquit ad eum: Accelera et excita omnes fratres, et ut velociter surgant, atque ad ecclesiam pergant, magnis clamoribus insta, quia haec, in qua quiescunt, cella sub omni est celeritate casura. Ille autem jussis obtemperans, magnis vocibus clamare coepit: Surgite, inquiens, fratres, surgite, atque ex hac cella, quia protinus ruitura est, quantocius exite, ne moram in ea amplius facientes, a ruinis, quod absit, opprimamini. Cum igitur illi expergefacti, ejus a clamoribus turbati, unde haec nosset inquirerent, ille quae viderat, quaeve sibi dicta fuerant ordine retulit. Mox itaque fratres, inde celeriter exeuntes, ecclesiam intraverunt, nocturnamque synaxim more solito, pulsatis signis, Domino decantare coeperunt. Cumque intentis mentibus officia consueta persolverent, subito praedicta domus, dato magno strepitu, funditus corruit. Exterriti fratres festine pergunt, solliciti ne quis eorum illa ruina oppressus esset inquirere: et cum delapsam materiam huc illucque devolverent, invenerunt unum e fratribus senectute gravatum sub ruinis undique circumjacentibus incolumem remansisse, extractumque foras quonam modo evasisset curiose interrogaverunt. At ille: Cum domus, inquit, funditus fatiscens super me dilaberetur, subito quidam splendidus vir, monastica veste indutus, mihi adstitit, ipsamque ruinam jamjamque super me ruentem, meque opprimere minitantem, brachio sustentans, incolumem, ut ipsi cernitis, conservavit. Qui videlicet beatus Benedictus fuisse creditur, qui et antea paterna pietate Dominicum gregem sub suo magisterio militantem sua admonitione et protectione eripuit, et senem fugere non valentem manu sollicitudinis suae defendit.

Quidam etiam frater in eodem monasterio Joannes dicebatur, qui aetate ac aegritudine pressus, extremum vitae spiritum trahebat. Cum igitur quadam die aliqui ex fratribus more solito decantaturi matutinas laudes ad eum venissent, ille eos voce qua potuit compescuit, dicens: Nolo, inquit, ut mihi canonicas horas amplius decantetis, quia dominus abbas cum multis fratribus albis vestibus indutis ad me modo gratia visitandi venerunt, mihique matutinale officium decantantes post paululum se huc venturos, meque secum assumpturos esse dixerunt. Dum itaque fratres qui ad eum venerant, ad ejus visionem intenti, et si vera essent quae retulerat, sollicite praestolarentur, post unius horae spatium frater ille magna cum exsultatione emisit spiritum. Ex quo animadvertere possumus B. P. Benedictum fuisse, qui ei cum illa albatorum concione apparuit, eumque secum, ut promiserat, assumpsisse. Haec quae retuli, in quadam veteri paginula imperito satis stylo exarata reperi, nostroque nunc associare libello studui.

Quia vero omnipotens Deus non tantum in magnis, sed etiam in minimis rebus aliquando ostendit mirabilia sua, ut fides credentium magis ac magis augeatur, ac in laudibus Creatoris sui universa creatura prorumpat, cum in cunctis usui humano concessis paterna pietate curam habere conspicitur. Quid de lampadibus in hac ecclesia nostris temporibus actum sit, sicut a Gregorio venerabili monacho, qui ejusdem ecclesiae custos adhuc superest, didici, ex parte referre non negligam.

Cum quadam die unus e custodibus lampadem in oratorio ante altare, igne admoto, accendisset, eamque sursum pene usque ad laquearia elevasset, repente delapsa, ante altare in pavimentum cecidit. Mirabilis Deus in factis suis! non solum fracta non est, sed nec oleum effusum, nec ignis in ea accensus exstinctus est.

Alio tempore cum praefatus Gregorius lampadem ante imaginem Salvatoris, quae supra fores ecclesiae depicta erat, vellet reficere, invenit eam extensis uncinulis ita in aere dependere, ut nulla prorsus materia sustentaretur. Qui mox convocatis fratribus, qui prope astabant, eis ut tanti testes miraculi esse deberent, quod miratur, ostendit.

Praeterea alio tempore in hac eadem ecclesia beati Benedicti ea nocte, quae praecedebat diem, qua ejus festivitas agebatur, sicut ab eis qui huic miraculo interfuere, accepi; dum ad vigilias unus e custodibus lampadem ante imaginem ejusdem beati Benedicti, reficeret, repente delapsa in pavimentum corruit, ac illaesa permansit: quae iterum ter sursum elevata, ter cecidit: et, quod mirabilius est, nec ipsa frangi, nec oleum effundi, nec lumen in ea accensum exstingui, divina conservante virtute, potuit.

Plura sunt in hujus monasterii oratorio ex lampadibus hujusmodi facta miracula: quae quia valde simplicia sunt, superfluum scribere duximus. Haec autem idcirco scripsimus, ne, quia parva sunt, omnino contemni viderentur. Unum autem, quod in superiori libro a memoria excidit, suo in ordine referre, in quo me tibi narrare promiseram, qualiter omnipotens Deus hoc monasterium saepe de tyrannorum manibus eripuerit, in hoc secundo, ne a memoria laberetur, scribere opportunum duximus.

Dum praedecessoris nostri Athenulphi tempore praedia hujus monasterii acriter ab Aquinensi comite infestarentur, et neque monachorum precibus, neque reverentia almi P. Benedicti qui fundator ac aedificator hujus coenobii exstiterat, animus ejus emolesceret, ut ab hujus loci laesione se aliquo modo temperaret, praedictus abbas necessitate compulsus, postquam vidit ferocem viri animum nullo modo mitigari posse, aliquot ex Nortmannis, qui tunc temporis conductu nostrorum principum Italiam adventabant, in possessiones hujus monasterii, quatenus eas a praedicto comite per eos tueretur, induxit. Qui postquam et domos ad manendum, et stipendia, quibus sustentarentur, abunde percepere, coeperunt quaeque monasterii pertinentia, more strenuorum militum, inimicis longe repulsis, circumcirca nobiliter fideliterque defendere. Igitur cum praedictus abbas, et qui ei in regimine secundo gradu successerat, supervixere, conducti milites satis honeste in eorum fidelitate manserunt: postquam vero ipsis hac vita subtractis, fortuna nostrorum principum mutata, aliquantulum vacillare coepit, Nortmannica cohors, quae ob nostram defensionem admissa fuerat, nobis infida atque adversa paulatim esse coepit; quae quotidie ad nostram perniciem ut canis et serpens, modo haec modo illa nobis auferens, ad dominationem sui juris sacrilega ducti cupiditate, devolvunt. Unde factum est ut ex tanta tamque ampla possessione nihil aliud ad nostri commodi usus, praeter civitatem, quae ad radicem Casini montis sita est, cum quatuor vel quinque villarum fundis, remanserit: qui etiam (sicut barbarica avaritia nescit tenere modum) quotidie ab eis oppressi, illis opes auferentes nobis miseriam atque inopiam tribuebant. Cum igitur per aliquanti spatium temporis sine ulla animi pietate id incessanter agerent, et misericors ac pius Dominus servis suis fame atque inopia laborantibus, sua benignitate subvenire decrevisset, beatissimus P. Benedictus cuidam rustico in agello cujusdam nostrae villulae commoranti, per visionem apparuit, eique ut egrediens se sequeretur jussit. Cumque idem rusticus ad eamdem visionem animum intenderet, visum est ei quod beatissimus Benedictus cunctos Nortmannos, qui ejus bona invaserant, cum virga, quam manu gestabat, potenti virtute a finibus hujus terrae expelleret, eosque vacuos rebus, oneratosque ignominia a sui haereditate monasterii eliminaret. Eodem itaque anno praefata cohors Nortmannica, amplius quam solebat per audaciam insolescens, ad nostram calamitatem, arcem, quae S. Andreae nuncupatur, ut securius nobis sublata retinere posset, occupavit: quae utique res illorum animum ad dominationem, nostrum ad desperationem adduxit. Postquam ergo eadem arce potiti sunt, quadam die in unum conglobati, magna cum superbia in praefatam Casini civitatem venientes intraverunt: ibique nutu Dei a populo civitatis oppressi, aliquanti eorum vel occisi vel capti sunt, caeteri autem qui remanserunt, in munitionem praedictae arcis fugientes se contulerunt, Igitur habitatores hujus terrae unanimiter facto grege, vicinis undique auxiliantibus, ad obsidionem ejusdem arcis animum intendunt. (Mira dicturus sum) obsidione facta, dum jacula ex utraque parte acriter impulsa mitterentur, Nortmannorum pila, velut a ventorum flamine retorta, eos a quibus missa fuerant, sauciabant. Quid multis opus est? cum se a semetipsis ita impugnari conspicerent, et jam amplius resistere minime valerent, cernentes durum sibi esse contra stimulum calcitrare (et quod contra se divinam dexteram dimicare cognoscerent) facta deditione in manibus abbatis et monachorum se tradunt: a quibus vix defensi ad socios, qui in Aversano oppido commorabantur, remissi sunt. Sicque factum est ut ab eo tempore, beati Benedicti meritis, haec in qua degimus terra ab eorum infestatione illaesa permaneat, atque sub ipsius sancti tutamine secura persistat.

Modus libelli hujus nos ad finem tendere cogit. Sed bonum obedientiae quae inter caeteras virtutes prima est, non sinit nos virtutem cujusdam fratris, qui eam tota cordis humilitate usque ad mortem quoque sectatus est, penitus silentio praeterire: illum videlicet imitans, qui factus obediens Patri usque ad mortem (Philipp. II), obedientiae nobis pariter ac patientiae reliquit exemplum.

Qui videlicet frater hujus nostrae congregationis Raynerius nomine, juvenis quidem aetate, sed moribus grandaevus fuit: cui multi ex fratribus, qui adhuc supersunt, et eum optime noverunt, testimonium perhibent, quod tantae humilitatis tantaeque obedientiae fuerit, ut ex hoc mirabilis ab omnibus haberetur.

Cui dum quadam die esset ab abbate suo injunctum, ad aliquod opus pro utilitate monasterii peragendum, Teatinum adire territorium, ille laeto, ut semper, animo ad obedientiam promptus, jussa implere festinans, iter arripuit. Qui dum pergeret, et aliquanti jam itineris spatium profligasset, a latrunculis cujusdam potentis viri Oderisii, qui ex praecepto ejus, si quid ex monasterii hujus rebus diripere possent, viam observabant, omnibus quae deferebat sublatis, interfectus est. Cujus quidem corpus, vel propter inimicorum insidias, vel quia longe erat, ad hoc coenobium deferri non potuit, sed in quadam ecclesia juxta posita humi traditum est. Sed quantum illius obedientia omnipotenti Deo fuerit accepta, ad exstinctum ejus corpus ostendere est dignatus. Coeperunt itaque multi infirmitate detenti ad ejus sepulcrum properare, et recepta sanitate ad sua incolumes remeare. Inter quos Atto comes, magni Attonis comitis filius, praefati quoque Oderisii gener, cum graviter detentus a febribus fatigaretur, ad sepulcrum istius, fama ducente, venit, ibique in oratione prostratus recedente febre ita sanus surrexit ut malae illius valetudinis, qua antea laborabat, nihil prorsus in se sentiret; qui pro recepta sanitate gratias referens, ob retributionem tanti muneris, optimo super ejus sepulcrum oblato pallio, gaudens discessit.

Et quoniam de mirabilibus Dei coepimus facere mentionem, quod mihi ipsi contigit, silentio praetereundum non duxi, dicente Scriptura quod Secretum regis abscondere bonum est, opera vero Dei manifestare ac revelare honorificum est (Tob. XII). Cum, intra annos pueritiae positus, vi febrium laborarem, beatae memoriae Joannes, reverendae dignitatis sacerdos, qui tunc in nostra Beneventana urbe in Dei servitio celebris habebatur, visitationis gratia ad me properans venit. Cumque paululum cum caeteris qui advenerant consedisset, et me vehementius a tertiano typo urgeri conspiceret, motus charitate quam erga me habebat, surrexit, ac perfusus ora lacrymis lenta voce Dominum invocans, manum capiti meo imposuit, et febris, quae me acrius infestabat, mox effugata discessit.

Ea etiam, quae Leone abbate monasterii S. Pauli apostoli, secundo ab urbe Roma milliario constituti, ubi sacratissimum ejus corpus signis prodigiisque coruscans veneratur et colitur, referente cognovi, in calce hujus libelli scribere curabo. Dicebat enim quod sibi Adam reverendissimus valde monachus et custos ecclesiae hujus nostri monasterii retulerit quia quadam die, dum idem venerabilis Adam portam monasterii ad aliquod opus faciendum esset egressus, duo juvenes in habitu monachi sibi in ipso introitu monasterii obviaverunt: cumque salutatos eos studiose qui essent inquireret, audivit ab eis quod unus eorum Protus, alter vero Hyacinthus diceretur. At ille, obstupefactus, cur venissent cum percunctaretur, illi inquiunt: Ad fratres, qui hodie nostri memoriam mente devota recolunt, visitandos venimus. Erat enim ea dies qua, pro Christo effuso sanguine, palmam martyrii ipso donante meruerunt. Cum ergo attonitus paululum substitisset, ac illi coepto itinere monasterium essent ingressi, ad se reversus, certius quod audierat cognoscere volens, rapido eos cursu prosequitur. Dumque eos huc illucque per monasterium studiose requireret, ac minime invenire posset, quosque sibi obviantes interrogare coepit ubi essent monachi qui modo secum loquentes monasterium essent ingressi? Sed illi nullum in monasterium introisse praeter illum se audisse professi sunt. Qua de re aperte datur intelligi, eos qui sibi apparuerant, sanctos Martyres Protum et Hyacinthum, quorum festivitas eo die celebrabatur, veraciter fuisse. Quae omnia eodem ordine a Firmo hujus monasterii veterano monacho, nepote scilicet ipsius Adae, quo ille mihi Romae positus dixerat, reversus ad monasterium, acta fuisse percepi.

Hic finem faciat hujus diei oratio: quatenus in honore tantorum martyrum liber iste conclusus, recreato per hujus noctis spatium animo, ad caetera quae restant sanctorum Acta, ipsorum omniumque sanctorum precibus adjuti, fideliter enarrando veniamus.

LIBER TERTIUS Qui est de miraculis alibi gestis. Expletis duobus, Christi gratia comitante, libellis, quos de miraculis Dei, vel in hoc coenobio, vel in sibi subditis cellis, ipso largiente patratis descripsimus, ad narrationem tertii concedente Domino veniamus. Et quia caetera, quae extra hujus monasterii claustra facta sunt, quaeque visu vel auditu percepimus, in aliis duobus libellis adhuc exaranda remanent, operae pretium mihi videtur ab ipso capite Ecclesiae exordium sumere, sicque postea seriatim stylo prosequente ad singula membra venire.

Dum igitur negligentia sacerdotum Italia a recto religionis tramite paulatim devians labefactaretur, in tantum mala consuetudo adolevit, ut sacrae legis auctoritate postposita divina humanaque omnia miscerentur, adeo ut populus electionem, et sacerdotes consecrationem, donumque sancti Spiritus, quod gratis accipere et dare divina auctoritate statutum fuerat, data acceptaque per manus pecunia ducti avaritia venderent; ita vix aliquanti invenirentur qui, non hujus Simoniacae pestis contagione foedati, mundi coram Deo praecepta Dominica observantes existerent. Itaque cum vulgus clericorum per viam effrenatae licentiae nemine prohibente graderetur, coeperunt ipsi presbyteri ac diacones (qui tradita sibi sacramenta Dominica mundo corde castoque corpore tractare debebant) laicorum more uxores ducere, susceptosque filios haeredes testamento relinquere; nonnulli etiam episcoporum verecundia omni contempta, cum uxoribus domo simul in una habitare. Et haec pessima et exsecranda consuetudo intra Urbem maxime pullulabat, unde olim religionis norma ab ipso apostolo Petro ejusque successoribus ubique diffusa processerat.

Igitur dum per aliquot annos nonnulli solo nomine pontificum cathedram obtinerent, Benedictus quidam nomine, non tamen opere, cujusdam Albenici consulis filius (Magi potius Simonis, quam Simonis Petri vestigia sectatus) non parva a parte in populum profligata pecunia, summum sibi sacerdotium vindicavit; cujus quidem post adeptum sacerdotium vita quam turpis, quam foeda, quamque exsecranda exstiterit, horresco referre; eo potius qualiter omnipotens Deus in faciem Ecclesiae sit dignatus respicere, exordiar enarrare. Denique cum rapinas, caedes, aliaque nefanda in Romanum populum aliquanta per tempora, sine ulla dilatione ageret, congregati in unum populi quia ejus nequitiam amplius ferre nequibant, eum a pontificatus cathedra exturbantes, Urbe pellunt; alterumque in loco ejus, Joannem videlicet Sabinensem episcopum (non tamen vacua manu) canonica parvipendentes decreta, substituunt; qui tribus non amplius mensibus Romanae usus est cathedrae successione, Benedicto undique suis cum propinquis infestante Urbem; quia ex consulibus terrae ortus erat, et in eis maxima virtus, Urbe cum dedecore pulsus, suum ad episcopatum reversus est. Benedictus igitur quod amiserat sacerdotium recepit, pristinos tamen mores minime mutavit, secundum quod scriptum est: Adolescens juxta viam suam; etiam cum senuerit, non recedet ab ea (Prov. XXII). Et quia durum est in corde veteri nova meditari, in eisdem pravis et perversis operibus, ut ante, perseverabat. Cumque se a clero simul et populo propter nequitias suas contemni respiceret, et fama suorum facinorum omnium aures impleri cerneret, tandem reperto consilio (quia, voluptati deditus, ut Epicurus magis quam ut pontifex vivere malebat) cuidam Joanni archipresbytero, qui tunc in Urbe religiosior caeteris clericis videbatur, non parva ab eo accepta pecunia, summum sacerdotium relinquens tradidit; ipse vero in propriis se castellis recipiens, Urbe cessit. Interea Joannes, cui Gregorius nomen inditum est, cum duobus annis et octo mensibus sacerdotium administrasset, Henricus rex, qui tunc Germaniae, Pannoniae, Saxoniae ac Italiae imperabat, ad suscipiendam de manu Romani pontificis imperialem coronam, quatenus deinceps Augustus appellari posset, Italiam ingressus, Romanam adiit urbem (anno 1047). Sed antequam Urbem ingrederetur, plurimorum episcoporum, nec non abbatum, clericorum quoque ac religiosorum monachorum, in Sutrina urbe concilio congregato, Joannem, qui Gregorius dictus est, missis ad eum episcopis, ut de ecclesiasticis negotiis, maximeque de Romana tunc Ecclesia, quae tres simul habere pontifices videbatur, ipso praesidente, tractaretur, venire rogavit. Sed haec de industria agebantur, jam enim dudum regio animo insederat ut tres illos, qui injuste apostolicam sedem invaserant, cum consilio et auctoritate totius concilii juste depelleret, et unus qui secundum statuta SS. Patrum Dominico gregi sollicite praeesset, clero et populo eligente, ordinaretur. Praedictus itaque pontifex exoratus a rege, caeterisque pontificibus, Sutrium, ubi synodus congregata erat, allectus spe quod, aliis duobus depositis, sibi soli pontificatus confirmaretur, gratanter perrexit. Sed postquam eo ventum est, et res agitari ac discuti a Synodo coepta est, agnoscens se non posse juste honorem tanti sacerdotii administrare, ex pontificali sella exsiliens, ac semetipsum pontificalia indumenta exuens, postulata venia, summi sacerdotii dignitatem deposuit.

Post haec rex Urbem ingressus, congregato in ecclesia B. Petri apostoli Romano clero et populo, una cum episcopis qui in praedictam convenerant synodum, communi consilio Clementem Bambergensem episcopum elegerunt, quia in Romana Ecclesia non erat tunc talis reperta persona quae digne posset ad tanti honorem sufficere sacerdotii: eumque in apostolica sede ad regendum Dominicum gregem inthronizantes constituunt. Quo non amplius novem mensibus sacerdotio functo, ex hac vita decedente, Damasus ex Germania oriundus, fultus auctoritate regia, eidem succedens, sacerdotium est adeptus, quique non amplius quam viginti et tribus diebus sacerdotio administrato diem clausit extremum. Huic successit Leo, de quo nobis est sermo prae manibus, vir per omnia apostolicus, regali genere ortus, sapientia praeditus, religione conspicuus, omnique ecclesiastica doctrina apprime eruditus, ac qui (quemadmodum scriptum est) coepit invocare nomen Domini; quemque etiam vidi ejusque familiaritatem habere merui: saepe etiam eo in ecclesia missas celebrante, cum illo ad divinum altare sacris indutus vestibus steti, eique Evangelium legi. A quo omnia ecclesiastica studia renovata ac restaurata, novaque lux mundo visa est exoriri.

Hic saepe sacerdotale consilium advocans, sacerdotes, diaconos et reliquos clericos non regulariter ordinatos removit, et in eorum locis ad veri et summi Dei cultum qui digne ministrare possent constituit. Quotidie quoque per se suosque discipulos ubique missos, populis viam Domini, litteris et verbis praedicans ostendebat. Qui per apostolicam viam semper gradiens, apostolicos etiam viros in miraculis est imitatus. De quo quidem plura audire me contigit, sed multis occupatus negotiis, singula quaeque discurrere non valens, pauca referre de pluribus satagam, ut per haec quanti vir iste meriti fuerit, quicunque in posterum legerit agnoscat.

Gregorii itaque pontificis, qui ab eo educatus ac subdiaconus ordinatus, nunc autem in Romana Urbe culmen apostolicum tenens, Christi Ecclesiam verbis simul et exemplis illustrat, didici relatione quae narro. Cujus utique verbis ita me credere oportet, ac si ego impraesentiarum adfuissem oculisque vidissem. Dum quodam tempore praedictus Leo venerabilis pontifex ecclesiasticis intentus negotiis in Gallia moraretur, a quodam abbate monasterii, sancti confessoris Christi Remigii lignarium poculum benedictionis causa oblatum, suscepit; quod videlicet, pro amore tanti pontificis valde diligebat, ac in eo refectionis hora in mensa sedens, aureis et argenteis posthabitis, bibere consueverat. Igitur dum quadam die ad mensam sedenti pincerna ex more poculum vellet porrigere, qua nescio negligentia tenentis de manu cecidit, moxque confractum in partes est. Cum denique beatissimus papa bis terque vinum requireret, et pincerna hac de causa venire differret, nuntiatum est ei quod poculum in quo bibere consueverat, de manu ferentis decidisset, fractumque fuisset; quod ille audiens valde tristatus est, non tantum damno scyphi, quantum quod vase de monasterio S. Remigii, benedictionis causa accepto, se frustratum cernebat, sibique astantibus: Fractum, mihi, inquit, scyphum afferte. Cumque sibi allatum fuisset, cernens utramque fracturam, omnipotentem Dominum deprecatus est ut meritis B. Remigii fractum sibi scyphum, quem pro amore ejus tantopere diligebat, restitueret. Moxque alteram partem alteri adjunxit, sicque eodem momento solidatus est ut nullum in eo, quod fractus fuisset, indicium remaneret, cunctis qui aderant admirantibus, ac in ejus veneratione acclamantibus. Ille non suis hoc, sed B. Remigii meritis imputare coepit, cujus de monasterio, charitatis gratia, id munus acceperat.

Theophilus. In hoc utriusque, alteriusve miraculo, illud B. P. Benedicti de re licet dissimili, similiter audio, primum renovari miraculum, dum in partes divisum rejunxit capisterium. (Greg. lib. II, Dialog.)

Desiderius. Interim te, charissime frater, silere oportet, quatenus intentus animo ad haec de illo majora cognoscas. Alio itaque tempore (sicut mihi praefatus papa Gregorius retulit) quidam Galliarum episcopus, ab eodem pontifice Leone fuerat episcopi honore suspensus; cujus quidam presbyter, Gibertus nomine, facundus sermone, et litteris haud mediocriter eruditus, eidem promiserat episcopo se Romam venire, atque callidis suis assertionibus eumdem beatum pontificem decipere, eique sublatum officium restitui impetrare: sicque ab eo accepta pecunia, Romam venit. Cumque se beatissimo pontifici praesentasset, coepit se huc illucque ut callidus serpens vertere, episcopum suum verbis rhetoricis excusare, blandis et humillimis precibus, ut interdictum officium injuste, ut asserebat, ablatum deberet restitui, flagitare. Sed cum id quod petebatur, sibi denegatum fuisset, nec eum ut speraverat, decipere posset, ne ad episcopum suum, a quo non parvam acceperat pecuniam, sine effectu reverti videretur, aliud exquisivit ingenium: adiit apostolicae sedis cancellarium, eique oblato pretio persuasit ut sibi furtivas litteras, et apostolico sigillo signatas, ad suum episcopum deferendas tribueret, quae et episcopale officium et gratiam apostolicae sedis sibi redditam significarent. Quae res beatum Leonem minime latuit, moxque praedictum presbyterum advocans, accepta quam obtulerat pecunia, eique in manum mittens, dixit: Pecunia tua tecum sit in perditionem, quia donum Dei furtim tentasti pecuniis possidere (Act. VIII). Cujus sermonem divina ultio mox secuta est, ita ut amissa mente ab illa die usque nunc ubique vagabundus incedat, nec ulla domus vel claustra ultra duos vel tres dies eum valeant retinere.

Qua de re aperte datur intelligi quod quisquis temerario ausu vel decipere vel ad iracundiam provocare tentaverit eum, qui in justis habitat procul dubio Dominum offendit: cujus et vindicem iram in se sentiat, quam non expertam temere devitare neglexerat.

Theophilus. Ita est ut asseris, sed, quaeso te, de virtute tanti Patris, si qua adhuc occurrunt animo, incunctanter prosequere.

SERMON AT THE COUNCIL OF BENEVENTO

Desiderius. Dum beatissimus pontifex Leo quinque per annos divinitus sibi concessum sacerdotium pie ac religiosissime administraret, ab hac instabili luce ad Christum, qui vera et aeterna lux est, coelorum laetantibus civibus, angelicis subvectus manibus commigravit. Et illi quidem paradisus patuit sanctorum recepto consortio. Sed infelix mundus, qui talem pontificem diu habere non meruit. Cujus post obitum multa et magna ad ejus tumulum aliisque in locis per eum Domino tribuente claruere miracula. E quibus omissis caeteris duo tantum (quia ad aliorum gesta narranda festino) aedificationis gratia huic libello subnectam.

Victor papa, qui in regimine sacerdotali ei successerat (sicut a veridicis viris nobis relata sunt) audita fama miraculorum ejus, quod per eum Dominus talia operaretur, fidem non accommodabat. Sed quia, ut ait Apostolus: Linguae in signum sunt non fidelibus sed infidelibus (I Cor. XIV), Omnipotens Dominus experimento eum docere voluit quae, audita a pluribus, minime credere volebat.

Curiensis quidam episcopus cujus nomen e memoria excidit, cum supra memorato pontifice Victore a Germania veniens, ejus in obsequio Romae morabatur; hic puerum ab utero matris mutum habebat, quem pro mercede animae suae pascens ac vestiens, quocunque ibat secum ducere consueverat, in cujus vacuo ore nec indicium quidem linguae inesse videbatur. Qui etiam episcopus ex mirabilibus ad B. Leonis tumulum patratis, similiter ut papa, incredulum animum gerebat. Cum igitur quadam die ad sedem sui episcopatus, jam accepta licentia, reverti decrevisset, ecclesiam B. Petri apostoli orationis gratia ingressus, postquam B. Petro se attentius commendavit suis cum clientibus, equis ascensis, puero in eadem ecclesia oblito, festinus viam quae eum ad suam ducebat patriam, egressus Urbe, gradiebatur. Cum itaque longiuscule adhuc esset ab Urbe profectus repente ei in memoriam rediit quod mutum puerum in ecclesia B. Petri reliquisset. Qui mox substitit, ac famulos suos, a quibus puer reduci deberet, quosdam remisit. Igitur cum illi apostolorum principis basilicam essent ingressi, conspiciunt puerum ante tumulum B. Leonis stantem, atque cum his qui circumstabant loquentem. Illis itaque mirantibus et qualiter hoc sibi evenisset quaerentibus, puer inquit: Postquam dominus meus hac in ecclesia me relinquens discessit, huc ad sepulcrum B. Leonis me contuli, si forte omnipotens Dominus officium, quo carebam, vocis meritis ejus mihi restituere dignaretur. Nec sum meo, quod corde poscebam, voto fraudatus, sed mox ut ante ejus venerandam memoriam lacrymans aliquantulum prostratus jacui, illico recepta voce loquens, ut ipsi videtis, surrexi. Ab illa itaque die, quod mirabilius est, coepit in ore ejus lingua, quae defuerat, paulatim crescere, ita ut intra paucos dies pleno ore linguam perfecte reciperet, et verba sine impedimento sonaret. Denique qui missi fuerant curaverunt puerum ad episcopum ducere, et quem tacentem reliquerat, beati Leonis suffragantibus meritis ei loquentem adducunt. Regressus igitur episcopus Romanum pontificem adiit, et quid omnipotens Dominus per B. Leonem operari dignatus fuisset, ostendit. Ex tunc coeperunt ipsi ejus veneranda merita cunctis praedicare, quae aliis antea referentibus non patiebantur audire.

Theophilus. Placent quia mira sunt, sed magis quia nova sunt.

Desiderius. Illustris vir Maximus, Romanae urbis civis, nuper retulit mihi de eodem venerabili praesule quae narro. Bernardus quidam pessimae mentis miles exstitit, qui apostolicae sedi contrarium se in omnibus quibus potuit modis exhibebat. Sed in bello quod a vicinis circa Urbem manentibus, conjurantibus cum Cadaloo Parmensi episcopo qui tunc apostolicam sedem invadere tentabat, cum militibus qui Romanam Ecclesiam defendebant commissum est, justo Dei judicio confossus interiit. Hic igitur, audita fama miraculorum quae omnipotens Deus meritis beati Leonis fidelibus populis exhibebat, non solum non credebat, verum etiam ore sacrilego deridebat et blasphemabat. Cum denique quadam die in conventu appareret populi, et sermo inter eos de signis et virtutibus beati Leonis exortus esset, coepit irridere dicens: Si sanctus est, ut dicis, contrahat mihi digitum meum, cumque compesceretur ab iis qui astabant, ne de sancto viro talia loqueretur, dimisso conventu discessit. Cum ecce forte canis qui eum sequebatur, suem in platea inventum invasit. Ille vero ne porcus disciperetur, festine cucurrit, et injecta manu canem tenere voluit; sed mox porcus hianti ore digitum ejus momordit, sicque ab illa die omni tempore quo vixit digitum contractum habens, nullatenus eum extendere potuit. Unde factum est ut qui Dei famulum irridere praesumpserat, ipse, contracto digito, omnibus derisui haberetur. Haec de tanto Patre B. Leone dicta sufficiant, ut, quia ad aliorum narranda gesta properamus, alii, cui otium est, quae multa de illo et mirabiliora dicuntur, scribenda relinquamus.

Quod Dominus in Evangelio dicit: Pater meus usque modo operatur, et ego operor (Joan. V, 17), quotidie cernimus adimpleri, et antiqua novis temporibus miracula innovari. Haec itaque quae dicturus sum adeo clara sunt, ut non solum in Florentina dioecesi, in qua facta noscuntur, verum etiam in tota Tuscia, ac in urbe, quae caput mundi est, Roma constet esse notissima.

Petrus quidam clericus est, qui occulte data pecunia regio adminiculo in praedicta Florentina civitate cathedram episcopatus accepit. Cum denique a clericis et populo, ut episcopum decebat, benigne fuisset susceptus, post non multum spatium temporis fama per ejusdem episcopatus dioecesim increbuit quod, Simoniacae haeresis peste foedatus, quod gratis, Domino jubente, accipere et dare statutum est, pecunia mercatus fuerit. Cumque tam horrenda et tam exsecranda fama primitus ad religiosorum, dehinc ad aures vulgi pervenisset, coeperunt se plures ab ejus communione subtrahere: Romanoque pontifici quaecunque super hac re cognoverant, divino exardescente zelo, studuerunt intimare. Qui, episcoporum consilio congregato, eumdem episcopum, ut rem diligenter agnosceret, convocavit. Sed cum se synodo praesentasset, accusatoribus undique acclamantibus, sacramento sese purgare nitebatur. Cumque coram praesentibus res aliquantulum agitata fuisset, datae induciae sunt, ut per easdem forsitan inductus, divinum expavescens judicium, quod pertinaciter negabat humiliter confiteretur, quatenus ab aeterno non removeretur altari, si ab hoc praesenti, cui ministrare juste non poterat, se abstinuisset. Interim populus in duas dividitur partes, quarum altera, quae amorem Dei muneribus praeferebat, clericos et religiosos monachos, qui contra episcopum rem comprobandam susceperant; altera quae munera et favorem diligebat, episcopum est secuta. Cum crebro igitur inter se altercaretur populus, et altera alteri obstaret parti, in tantum exorta augebatur contentio, ut, inter se dimicantibus, saepe etiam usque ad effusionem sanguinis venirent. Cumque haec diutius agerentur, et neutra pars parti cederet, Joannes reverendissimus abbas monasterii quae Umbrosa Vallis dicitur, saepe ad hunc conflictum advocatus, zelo Dei ductus suis cum monachis veniebat, qui exhortando, praedicando, divini examinationem judicii intentando, episcopum admonere non cessabat quatenus ex perpetrata culpa poenitentiam ageret, et sacerdotio minime legaliter acquisito humiliter cederet, nec sibi suisque subjectis, quibus incremento esse debuerat, detrimento foret. Illud de Evangelio ei saepe proponens, quomodo Dominus Jesus vendentes et ementes columbas de templo projecerit, cathedrasque subverterit, et aes nummulariorum effuderit (Joan. II, 15), videlicet demonstrans ut quicunque Spiritus sancti donum, quod per columbam significatur, ductus avaritia, vel vana gloria elatus, pretio acquirere vel vendere tentaverit, ab illo coelesti templo et aeterno altari se procul dubio eliminandum noverit. Sed ille nihilominus praesentis vitae honoris cupidus pro nihilo monita sancti viri ducebat, imo potius pertinaciter et armis et verbis, omnibusque modis quibus poterat se defendere nitebatur. Cumque idem venerabilis abbas incassum procedere sua verba videret, utraque parte populi advocata: Quoniam, inquit, verba non prosunt, veniamus ad signa. Construatur rogus, et igne supposito accendatur, per quem unus e nostris ingrediatur, ut utrum vera an falsa sint quae de episcopo dicimus, Domino discernente, probetur. Placet utrique parti sententia: rogus mox duodecim pedum mensura construitur; intra quem parva semita, qua unius tantum hominis persona transire posset, relinquitur: quae etiam ex accensis lignis, ne ibi aliquis locus a flamma vacaret, consternitur. Interim autem dum haec praeparantur, praefatus abbas Joannes Petro suo discipulo, reverendissimo videlicet, viro, qui postmodum in Albanensi urbe episcopus ordinatus est, quique etiam adhuc superest eamdem Ecclesiam regens, praecepit ut indutus sacris vestibus omnipotenti Deo sacrificium offerret; et sic demum confisus de misericordia Dei per accensi rogi flammas indubitanter intraret.

Qui jussis Patris obtemperans, postquam sacrificium Deo obtulit, casulam se exspoliat, ad ignem venit, et magna voce: Oro, inquit, Deus omnipotens, si Petrus, qui episcopus dicitur, Simoniaca est peste foedatus, ne Ecclesia tua amplius polluatur, judicio S. Spiritus tui ostende virtutem: illaesum me per hunc ignem transire concede. Quod si nos fallacia pleni, causa invidiae ducti, hanc contra eum tulimus quaestionem, ardor istius ignis me tua gratia derelictum consumat. Haec dicens, et sanctae crucis se signaculo muniens, per medias flammas constanter ingressus est. Cum igitur undique esset flammis circumdatus, ita ut a nemine prorsus videretur, et omnes eum jam consumptum putarent, subito ex alia parte, Christi comitante gratia, egrediens prosilivit, ita ut non modo vestimenta ejus, sed ne capillus quidem laesus ab igne in aliquo videretur. Sed, ut idem venerabilis vir postea referebat, cum per medias flammas graderetur, mappula de manu ejus cecidit. Cumque jam pene egrederetur ex igne, vidit se mappulam in manibus non gestare, ac, in ignem sibi eam cecidisse considerans, per medias iterum flammas revertitur, et secum mappulam extrahens reportavit. Tunc omnes qui aderant, viso tam maximo, tam obstupescendo miraculo, immensas Deo gratias agentes, mox diversa pars una effecta, praefatum episcopum de ecclesia pellunt: qui postea poenitentia ductus, mutata veste, sub sanctae conversationis regula religiosam agere vitam visus est.

Theophilus. Ut laetando miror, et mirando laetor, quod mediocritatis nostrae tempore illud antiquum et gloriosum trium puerorum miraculum intueor, cum de camino aestuantis incendii integri et incorrupti toto corpore prodierunt.

Desiderius. Venerabilis Gregorius papa, cujus superius memoriam feci, quid contra eamdem Simoniacam haeresim, se praesente, Dominus ostendere voluit, saepe mihi solitus est referre. Cum essem, inquit, subdiaconus, et a beatae memoriae Victore hujus apostolicae sedis pontifice in Galliam pro ecclesiasticis negotiis discutiendis essem transmissus, curae mihi fuit episcoporum convocare concilium, ut illis coram positis de ecclesiasticis negotiis tractaremus. In eadem vero civitate in qua synodus agebatur, episcopus erat qui pretio honorem comparasse episcopatus a multis infamabatur. Igitur vocatus episcopus venit ad medium. Cum ergo eum exhortari salutaribus monitis coepissemus ut quaesibi opponebantur, conscientia jam fatente, humiliter confiteretur, ille, tum quia ejusdem civitatis erat episcopus, tum quia fretus auxilio comitis terrae ipsius, plenus superbia omnino verba nostra vilipendebat. Sed cum a nobis et a caeteris qui aderant episcopis sub justitiae regula se, quod non speraverat, constringi conspiceret, nec effugiendi haberet licentiam, negare pertinaciter coepit quod ante vix audire dignabatur. Cumque verba producerentur in longum, et maximum diei spatium esset consumptum, et ille nihilominus in sua pertinacia negando persisteret homo, eum cum caeteris qui aderant religiosis episcopis nobis adjurare visum fuit et totum judicium in ostensione Spiritus sancti committere. In nomine, inquam, Patris et Filii et Spiritus sancti, cujus donum gratiae te comparasse audivimus, ut hujus rei nobis veritatem edisseras adjuramus. Quod si amplius, ut coepisti, negare tentaveris, Spiritum sanctum, donec, quae vera sunt confitearis, nominare non valeas. Qui episcopus, cum abunde eloquens esset, et a nobis exoraretur ut Spiritum sanctum nominaret, Patrem quidem et Filium satis diserte nominabat, Spiritum vero sanctum mirum in modum nominare nullo modo poterat. Tunc omnibus qui aderant luce clarius patuit quod honorem episcopatus dato pretio emerat, qui nonnisi Spiritus sancti gratia largiente tribuitur. Tunc Spiritus sancti virtute tremefactus episcopus, humiliter coram omnibus confiteri coactus est quod ante, inflatus superbia Dei, timore postposito procaciter negare praesumpserat.

Theophilus. Cum Pater, et Filius, et Spiritus sanctus unum sint, nec aliud de Patre et Filio quam de Spiritu sancto sentire fas est, cur in Patris et Filii vocabulis proferendis solutam atque disertam, in solo vero Spiritus sancti nomine, quasi praecellenti, linguam mutam et omnino habuit colligatam?

Desiderius. Justo Dei judicio contigit ut qui donum Spiritus sancti gratiae, quod gratis et datur et accipitur, lingua placitante mercatus est, in proferendo Spiritus sancti vocabulo specialiter linguae officium non haberet.

Alferius abbas monasterii Sanctae Trinitatis ab ipso in latere montis aedificati, qui inter Salernitanam et Amalphitanam civitates praeeminet mari, exstitit: cujus religiosam ac Deo amabilem vitam et ipse ex parte vidi, qui apud eum aliquantulum familiariter mansi, et aliis referentibus agnovi. Miraculum vero quod divina virtus in eo operari dignata est, quodque a quampluvimis didici, aequum est silentio non transire. Denique dum quadam pro utilitate monasterii Salernitanam urbem adiret per viam praecisi montis gradiens, deorsum cum equo quo sedebat per immane praecipitium cecidit: quod tanta altitudine mari superjacet, ut quinquaginta et eo amplius passus in altum praetendi videatur. Dum igitur qui cum eo pergebant illum sine dubio exstinctum putarent, nimium tristes et flentes, per quoddam diverticulum ad mare, si saltem illum aliquo modo invenire possent ut sepulturae traderent, descendere curaverunt. Cum autem sub radice montis, molles juxta littus maris calcantes arenas, festinanter ad locum quo ceciderat pergerent, invenerunt eum in via sanum et incolumem, equo cum quo ceciderat insidentem, Salernum propere coepto itinere tendere. Cumque illi, obstupefacti, qualiter res evenisset omnino nequirent perpendere, coeperunt Deo gratias agere, vocesque quasi tumultuantes in altum levare. Sed ab illo repente compressi praeceptum audiunt: Si meis, inquit, benedictionibus frui vultis, nulli, quandiu vixero, quae ex me vidistis dicatis.

Dicitur etiam de illo quod mortuum suscitaverit; quod videlicet illis qui eum ejusque vitam ad liquidum noverunt incredibile minime videtur.

Leo abbas, qui ei in monasterii regimine successit, sub ejus magisterio educatus ejus in obsequio praepositurae officium gerens, qui prae caeteris fratribus ei familiariter adhaerebat, nuper mihi retulit quia quodam tempore saeculares viri, ut ejus orationibus fruerentur, visitationis gratia ad ipsum venerunt. Quibus post spiritualem, corporalem etiam ejus refectionem praebere cupiens, praefato Leoni, suo videlicet praeposito, praecepit charitatis causa mensam eis apponere et prandium praeparare. Qui nihil aliud praeter panem et vinum, et quinque ova gallinacea, quod eis ad manducandum praebere posset, se habere respondit; sed qualiter inter eos ipsa ova dividi deberent, ignorare: erant illi utique septem. Cui ille: Festina, inquit, quantocius, et eadem ova igne adhibito praepara, mihique ut eis apponam deporta. Cucurrit ille et, sicut sibi fuerat imperatum, ova decoxit, eique, ut praeceperat, detulit. Qui accipiens, benedixit, et ex quinque ovis, septem viris, quod mirabile est, singulis singula praebuit.

Theophilus. Cum septem distributa hominibus sic augeri quinque ova considero, ut singuli singula aequali sorte accipiant, illud quodammodo miraculum video, quo Auctor omnium de quinque panibus quinque millia hominum saturavit (Matth. XVI, 9).

Desiderius. Amita patris mei, Bella nomine, in monasterio Beati Petri apostoli intra Beneventanam urbem posito, in sanctimoniali habitu a primaevo juventutis flore usque ad ultimam senectutem degit. Quae, cum esset desponsata viro, occulte de domo parentum fugiens ad monasterium contendit, ibique virginitatem suam omnipotenti Domino dicavit; et, quia terrenum in terra sponsum habere contempsit, procul dubio meruit habere coelestem in coelis. Ipsa mihi solita erat referre de abbatissa sua quae Offa dicebatur. Quae in monte qui Sanctae Agathae martyris dicitur, prope Capuanam urbem, antequam regimen monasterii susciperet, longo tempore habitaverit, ibique vitam eremiticam duxerit: dehinc monasterii suscepto regimine, quadam nocte sororibus adhuc quiescentibus oratorium ingressa accepit thuribulum, ut more solito thura adoleret altaribus. Cum itaque thus in thuribulum mittere vellet, e manu ejus cecidit et lampade a vento exstincta thus invenire non valuit.

Repente vero quidam juxta illum astitit, et tenens manum ejus, thymiama, quod in thuribulum posuerat, dedit. Tantus igitur odor ex illo incenso thymiamate emanavit, ut per totum quod reliquum erat noctis, usque ad horam diei tertiam non solum ecclesiam, sed etiam omne illud monasterium mira suavitate repleverit. Ex qua re sine dubio datur intelligi quod angelus Domini fuerit qui illud thymiama tanti fragrantiae odoris tribuerit.

Haec eadem religiosissima abbatissa, dum multa per tempora sollicite virginibus praefuisset, verbis et exemplis sibi commissas Dei famulas instruere non cessans, languore tacta corporis venit ad mortem. Cumque in extremo posita jam prope esset ut Christo, cui servierat, animam reddere deberet, videntibus cunctis qui aderant e lectulo se quasi ad mensuram trium cubitorum in aere elevans, expansis in coelum manibus stetit. Et facta oratione, iterum se in lectulo collocans, ultimum spiritum exhalavit. Sed ex hoc quantae fuerit abstinentiae dignosci potest. Quae dum infirma jaceret in lectulo, et a multis honestioribus viris ac mulieribus, visitationis gratia ad ipsam venientibus, ut aliquantulum cibi, quo infirmum corpus sustentaretur, caperet, rogaretur, illa desueta deliciis: Si aliquid, inquit, mihi de infusis leguminibus attuleritis, forsitan aliquantulum inde potero degustare. O abstinentia in femina praedicanda, quae, in infirmitate posita, infusis leguminibus pro summis etiam deliciis utebatur! Quae cum fuisset defuncta, et in ecclesia sepulta, quadam die rusticus quidam frumento onustus per eamdem ecclesiam transiens, supra sepulcrum ejus, parvipendens cujus meriti esset quae ibi sepulta jacebat, saccum cum frumento deposuit, et fessus, ut aliquantulum pausaret, juxta consedit. Repente igitur saccus divinitus de eodem sepulcro sublatus longeque projectus, omne illud, quo plenus erat, frumentum passim per eamdem ecclesiam sparsit. Rusticus ergo vehementer conterritus, ab illa die didicit quantum Dei homines in corpore venerandi sint; cum exstincta illorum corpora ac in sepulcro posita, ne ab aliquibus parvipendantur divina sibi virtus voluit demonstrare.

Alter quidam nobilis vir de eadem Beneventana urbe nescio qua causa monasterium adventarat, ac nescius, forte ejus supra sepulcrum consederat: cum subito tantus dolor viscerum eum invasit, ut, vociferans atque ejulans, se eadem hora moriturum putaret. Ad cujus vocem quae in monasterio erant virgines protinus cucurrerunt, eique cujus esset sepulcrum supra quod sederat indicaverunt. Qui, pro ignorantia venia postulata, meritis Dei famulae coelitus meruit medicinam.

In eadem urbe monasterium est quod Sanctae Sophiae dicitur, huic Casinensi monasterio subditum, in quo quidam a pueritia sanctae conversationis et magnae humilitatis monachus fuit, qui infra annos adolescentiae nimio tanguore praeventus ad extrema perductus est. Ad cujus exitum congregati fratres, hymnis et psalmis Deo coeperunt ejus animam commendare, sanctorumque coetus in ejus auxilium attentius invocare: qui crescente languore defunctus est. Sed dum ad lavandum ejus corpus aqua praeparatur, per unam fere horam exanimis jacuit. Cumque qui aderant orationi et psalmodiae insisterent, subito corpus ejus omne contremuit, ac paulatim reviviscens cunctis mirantibus in lectulo consedit. Dein, interrogatus, coepit illis quae egressus de corpore viderat referre, dicens: Cum anima mea, vobis litanias canentibus sanctosque Domini invocantibus, de corpore egrederetur, mox ad preces vestras sancti, quos invocastis, meum in auxilium advenerunt. Cumque illi ab eo requirerent si illos, quos nunquam viderat, cognoscere potuisset? Respondit: Sanctum Benedictum et sanctum Gregorium cognovi, B. Donatum et Felicem, cum reliquis qui in hac ecclesia requiescunt sanctis, meum in auxilium venire conspexi. Inter quos beatus Mercurius patronus noster velut splendidum sidus rutilans videbatur. Quem cum interrogassent utrumnam in hac vita esset moraturus? Minime, inquit: nam B. Mercurius hodie se ad me assumendum venire spopondit. Quae ut dixerat vera fuisse rei exitus comprobavit. Eodem namque die ex hac luce subtractus, ab illis procul dubio est receptus, quos antea moriens suum in auxilium venire conspexit. Ego denique in eodem monasterio positus, unum ex illis qui adfuerant testibus, Sicenolfum nomine, superstitem vidi, qui cuncta haec ut dicta sunt se vidisse et audivisse profitebatur.

The Scriptorium Project is the work of a small group of lay people of various apostolic churches who are interested in the preservation, transmission, and translation of the works of the early and medieval church. Our efforts are to make the works of the church fathers accessible to anyone who might have an interest in Christian antiquities and the theological, philosophical, and moral writings that have become the bedrock of Western Civilization.

To-date, our releases have pulled from the Greek, Nordic, Visigothic, Slavic, Armenian, Syriac, Georgian, Anglo-Saxon, Byzantine, Persian, German, Celtic, Ethiopian, and Coptic traditions of Christianity, and have been pulled from sundry local traditions and languages.

www.ingramcontent.com/pod-product-compliance
Lightning Source LLC
LaVergne TN
LVHW061038070526
838201LV00073B/5096